A Treasury of ʿĀ'ishah

THE TREASURY SERIES IN
ISLAMIC THOUGHT AND CIVILISATION

I. *A Treasury of Ḥadīth*, Ibn Daqīq al-ʿĪd

II. *A Treasury of al-Ghazālī*, Mustafa Abu Sway

III. *A Treasury of Sacred Maxims*, Dr. Shahrul Hussain

IV. *A Treasury of Ibn Taymiyyah*, Mustapha Sheikh

V. *A Treasury of Rūmī*, Dr. Muhammad Isa Waley

VI. *A Treasury of Iqbal*, Abdur Rashid Siddiqui

VII. *A Treasury of ʿĀ'ishah*, Sofia Rehman

Sofia Rehman

كنوز من عائشة

A TREASURY OF ʿĀ'ISHAH

A Guidance from the Beloved of the Beloved

KUBE PUBLISHING

A Treasury of ʿĀ'ishah

First published in England by
Kube Publishing Ltd
Markfield Conference Centre
Ratby Lane, Markfield
Leicestershire LE67 9SY
United Kingdom

TEL +44 (0)1530 249230

WEBSITE www.kubepublishing.com
EMAIL info@kubepublishing.com

CIP data for this book is available from the British Library.

ISBN 978-1-84774-201-8 casebound
ISBN 978-1-84774-202-5 ebook

Cover design by: Inspiral Design
Book design by: Imtiaze Ahmed
Arabic & English typesetting by: nqaddoura@hotmail.com
Printed by: Imak Offset, Turkey

Dedication

This book is dedicated to my beloved parents, Sajida Rehman and the late Mahmud Rehman.

رَّبِّ ٱرْحَمْهُمَا كَمَا رَبَّيَانِى صَغِيرًا ﴿٢٤﴾

(ألإسرآء ١٧ : ٢٤)

My Lord, have mercy on them, as they raised me when I was a child. (al-Isrāʾ 17: 24)

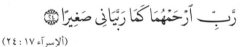

Transliteration Table

Arabic Consonants

Initial, unexpressed medial and final: ء ’

ا	a	د	d	ض	ḍ	ك	k
ب	b	ذ	dh	ط	ṭ	ل	l
ت	t	ر	r	ظ	ẓ	م	m
ث	th	ز	z	ع	ʿ	ن	n
ج	j	س	s	غ	gh	هـ	h
ح	ḥ	ش	sh	ف	f	و	w
خ	kh	ص	ṣ	ق	q	ي	y

with a *shaddah*, both medial and final consonants are doubled.

Vowels, diphthongs, etc.

Short:	ـَ	a	ـِ	i	ـُ	u
Long:	ـَا	ā	ـِي	ī	ـُو	ū
Diphthongs:			ـَوْ	aw		
			ـَيْ	ay		

بسم الله الرحمن الرحيم

Contents

Acknowledgements

My deepfelt gratitude to Yahya Birt, who, unbeknown to him, fulfilled a long-time wish of mine when he proposed that I should write a Treasury of ʿĀ'ishah bint Abu Bakr to contribute to the outstanding Treasury series. Thank you for your trust in me. I pray I have done the series justice.

Likewise, thank you to Kube Publishing and in particular to brother Haris Ahmad who remained patient and kind as I wrote this book during the tumultuous period of the unprecedented global lockdown of 2020.

I would like to thank Sabina Qadri, my dear friend and sister, for reading parts of the first draft of this book and giving me her invaluable feedback.

My heartfelt love and gratitude to my beautiful children: Yusuf, Ayesha, Khadija and Suleyman, who listened to me read sections aloud and gave me their thoughtful feedback. How blessed I am to have such wise little ones, *al-ḥamdulillāh*. In particular I must thank my daughter Ayesha who eagerly listened to and responded to each new statement and commentary. May Allah raise you to be like your namesake, *āmīn*. Deepest thanks also to my husband, Mustapha Sheikh; here's to our first "his and hers".

Words do not encompass the gratitude I wish to express to my mother Sajida Rehman, my brother Omar Rehman and my sister-in-law Leyla, who gave me the time, support and space to finish writing this book during one of the most difficult periods in our lives. My mother lost her husband, Mahmud Rehman, and we lost our father, just as I needed to finish this challenging task—your love and support made it possible. May the good of this book be a *ṣadaqat jāriyah* for daddy.

Finally, but most fervently, all praise and thanks are to Allah, who heard the *duʿā* of this undeserving servant and out of His infinite generosity said "Be" and so it was.

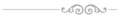

Introduction

۞ ۞ ۞

'Ā'ishah bint Abu Bakr ؓ is an icon among the giants of the first community of believers in Islam. She is famed as the daughter of Abu Bakr al-Ṣiddīq ؓ, the first Caliph of Islam, and as the most beloved wife of the Prophet Muhammad ﷺ. Whilst both of these positions earned her great esteem, she proved herself worthy of the elevated rank she acquired through her own intellectual inquisitiveness, piety, commitment to justice, compassion for the Muslim community, and absolute loyalty to Allah and His Messenger ﷺ.

This is not a biographical book on 'Ā'ishah bint Abu Bakr ؓ, though such a book would be important and timely; it is a collection of forty statements made by her, each being followed by my commentary based on years of research on 'Ā'ishah bint Abu Bakr ؓ rooted in the Qur'an, hadith, and the wider Islamic tradition. The book is divided into thematic sections: 'Ā'ishah's exegesis of the Qur'an (*tafsīr*); her jurisprudence (*fiqh*); matters pertaining to belief ('*aqīdah*); her political activism (*siyāsah*); and heart softeners *(al-raqā'iq)*. Each of these sections contains a varying number of statements.

The final section, 'At the First Sign of Hardship the Believer's Refuge is in Allah', stands alone and breaks away from the design of the rest of the book and, indeed, the rest of the Treasury series. It presents only one of ʿĀ'ishah's statements for which I then provide a lengthy explanation. This is because the statement refers to one of the most defining moments in ʿĀ'ishah's life: the *Ifk*, the slander that was promulgated by the hypocrites of Madinah in an attempt to defame our Mother ʿĀ'ishah and to bring hurt and injury of every sort to the blessed Messenger of Allah ﷺ. This event was deeply instructive for the first community of believers, and indeed all these centuries later it continues to be a source of instruction and inspiration. I hope, therefore, that the reader benefits from the extended attention granted to this statement.

I would like to acknowledge that when I began to write this book I was under the impression that it was the first of its kind, and in many ways it is; it is the first in the Treasury series to be written by a woman about a woman, it is also extensive in that it uses a range of sources beyond al-Bukhārī and Muslim, including history books such as *Tārīkh al-Ṭabarī* and works of exegesis such as Fakhr al-Dīn al-Rāzi's *al-Tafsīr al-Kabīr*, Ibn Kathīr's *Tafsīr al-Qur'ān al-'Aẓīm* and al-Qurṭubi's *al-Jāmi' li-Aḥkām al-Qur'ān* alongside other works that include more contemporary scholarship. It is not, however, the first time that forty hadith of ʿĀ'ishah ﵂ have been recorded in a single compilation. In 2018, Nurideen Knight self-published 40 *ḥadīth of Our Mother ʿAisha*. In this book she made the effort of compiling forty hadith narrated by ʿĀ'ishah bint Abu Bakr ﵁ from *ṣaḥīḥ al-Bukhārī* and *ṣaḥīḥ Muslim*. Though our two books are distinct in scope and form, the efforts of fellow Muslim women are too often overlooked and so I would like to ensure that readers are aware of and benefit from sister Nurideen Knight's book too.

ʿĀ'ishah bint Abu Bakr ﵁ has proven to be such an immense ocean of insight and wisdom for generations of Muslims that it is unlikely we could ever have too many books about her life and interventions. Her teachings and her example have much to offer not only for Muslim women but men too. It is a sad fact that books written by women about women are assumed to be exclusively for women, but I urge my brothers to pick this book up and follow in the footsteps of the Companions ﵃ in seeking out her wisdoms. Abu Burdah[1] ﵁ reports on the authority of his father who said, 'Whenever a Prophetic statement was difficult for us, the Companions, to understand we would ask ʿĀ'ishah [about it] and would find with her knowledge (i.e., understanding) about it.'[2] Masrūq[3] said, 'By Allah I witnessed the most senior of the Companions of Muhammad ﷺ ask her regarding [religious] obligations.' The *tābiʿī* al-Zuhri said, 'If you gathered together the knowledge of all the people including the Mothers of the Believers, ʿĀ'ishah would still be more extensive in knowledge [in comparison].'

It is my hope that this book allows readers of all backgrounds to take a sip from the fount of knowledge that is ʿĀʾishah bint Abu Bakr ☙.

May Allah grant us each the *tawfīq* to follow in the illuminated footsteps of our Mother ʿĀʾishah ☙, to show courage as she showed courage, to exert ourselves as she exerted herself in all that is beloved to Allah, to stand for truth as she stood for truth, to be of service to the community as she was of service, to elevate and practice the Word of Allah as she elevated and practiced the Word of Allah. *āmīn*.

I

Tafsīr of ʿĀ'ishah bint Abu Bakr ﵂

In the Mustadrak, al-Ḥākim al-Naysābūrī relays the following anecdote:

> One day, the first Umayyad Caliph, Muʿāwiyah asked a man in his entourage, 'Who is the most knowledgeable of all people?' Presumably calculating that giving a forthright answer might not be the most advantageous course of action, the man replied, 'Leader of the Believers, it is you!' But when the Caliph pressed him for a more honest response, he answered, 'Well, if you insist – then, it is ʿĀ'ishah.'[4]

The authority and knowledge of ʿĀ'ishah bint Abu Bakr ﵂ is undisputed, but sadly, as the above anecdote illustrates, it has often been deemed more gainful to overlook her opinion in favour of someone else's.[5] In this chapter the breadth of her knowledge is

presented as she demonstrates a multifaceted understanding of the Qur'an: she can speak to its context,
grammar, spirit, and theological philosophy. That
she is so profoundly dexterous in her understanding
of the Qur'an is a source of inspiration and clarity
for all Muslims.

The power of *duʿāʾ* and the nearness of Allah to the believer

> Never does a believer supplicate to Allah,
> except that they are either granted that *duʿāʾ*
> immediately in this world or that it is delayed
> until the afterlife, as long as they are not hasty
> or despairing.[6]

This statement by ʿĀʾishah ❊ is found in the exegeses
of Ibn Kathīr and al-Ṭabarī, for the beautiful verse
of the Qur'an wherein Allah ❊ states: *And when my
servants ask you about Me, then verily, I am near. I
respond to the supplication of the one who calls out
to Me, so ask of Me and believe in Me, so that they
may be rightly guided* (al-Baqarah 2: 186).

Upon hearing this statement, ʿUrwah ❊ asked,
'O Mother, what does it mean to be hasty or to despair?' She replied, 'It is to say, I asked, but was not
given, I supplicated but received no reply.'

For the believer in all of their states, whether
their life is flourishing during a season of success
and ascent or being tested by a season of difficulty

and hardship, there is hope and refuge to be found in this address by our Lord, and in the explanation given by our Mother. Allah ﷻ engages the first-person singular in the Arabic, أنا, indicating intimacy and nearness, instead of the first-person plural, نحن, that is also utilised by Allah to indicate His Might and Power, creating a physical proximity to His believing servant. It is Allah's way of having you, the attentive reader, feel Allah's nearness to you as you read this verse. But Allah does not stop at simply reminding us that He is near, He goes on to assert that He responds to the believer who has laid out their hands before their Creator to ask of Him alone, asserting no partners with Him, humbled and with a heart filled with hope and longing for Allah. And Allah does not stop there either. Allah then encourages us to ask and ask again, for indeed He is the One whose generosity knows no bounds (*al-Karīm*), the One who is eternally patient (*al-ṣabūr*) and therefore never irritated by the incessant asking of His creation, and He who loves to respond to all who call on Him (*al-Mujīb*).

The gifts of this verse do not end there, as finally Allah then reveals that the true fruit of asking from Him alone and believing in Him alone is that you will be rightly guided, because truly it is guidance in all our affairs that is the greatest blessing we can receive. This guidance can come in many forms, but the first of these is the strengthening of your relationship with Allah. Why would the One who is All-Knowing (*al-Khabīr*) need us to inform Him of our needs? Allah has of course no need for us to articulate our heart's innermost wishes, but in our turning to Allah and in our daily conversing with Him, it is *our* heart that is drawn closer to Allah, it is *our* soul that is replenished and given succour, and it is *our* faith that is strengthened by this reliance on none but Allah. This is the first, perhaps most valuable, response to our action of turning to Allah in supplication.

If we have the guidance of Allah, we have been granted the light with which we can travel through darkness, the rope which we can hold on to in order to be led in the right direction, the compass with which we navigate through life. Allah is generous and as our beloved Prophet Muhammad ﷺ told us, Allah is also shy and dislikes that a believing Muslim should spread their hands before Him and have them return empty.[7] With a Lord who tells us He is near, encourages us to ask and ask again, and who promises a response in addition to His guidance, how can we ever be hasty or despair of His Mercy?

Every hardship or suffering is an expiation for the believer

> Whenever a servant of Allah commits sinful acts, Allah will take them to account for it in this world through tests of hardship, sadness or pain, such that when they arrive in the next

> life, they will not be asked or punished for anything.[8]

This comment comes from ʿĀ'ishah's reflections on the verse by Allah ﷻ that says, *To Allah belongs whatever is in the heavens and in the earth, and whether you openly declare or conceal what is within you, Allah will take you to account. Allah may forgive whomsoever He Wills, and may punish whomsoever He Wills, and Allah is over all things, Powerful* (*al-Baqarah* 2: 284).

Similarly, al-Ṭabarī tells of a woman who was perturbed by the burden of this verse, fearful of being held to account for her every misdeed knowing that humans were created with a propensity to err. She came to ʿĀ'ishah ؓ and asked her about this verse. ʿĀ'ishah ؓ was taken back to a time when she too went to her beloved husband, the Prophet ﷺ with similar fears, and he allayed them telling her that this is the exchange of Allah with His believing servant. If one has not repented, then the hardships and difficulties that enter our lives may be because Allah, through His Infinite Mercy is protecting us from the evil we have committed against our own selves, and instead of causing us to be held to account on the Day of Judgement when accountability will weigh heavily upon us, our misdeeds are being mitigated in this life.

Who knows the intensity of tests, greater than our Mother, ʿĀ'ishah ؓ, who in the prime of her youth and in the comfort of the nurturing relationship of her doting husband, was suddenly thrust into an evil campaign of slander against her? The streets of Madinah were ablaze with rumours of the worst kind that questioned ʿĀ'ishah's integrity and fidelity. When she realised that even her loving husband had been brought to the precipice of doubt and that her parents too were fearful that the rumours may hold some truth, she resolutely turned to place her full reliance in Allah. It is reported that she said to the Prophet ﷺ that hers is 'the patience of Yaʿqūb',[9] a reference to the patience of Yūsuf's father whose heartbreak at the loss of his son led him to go blind from all the tears he had shed, but whose heart remained firm in the reliance and trust that Allah would return his most favoured son to him. Just as Yaʿqūb's patience was rewarded, so too was ʿĀ'ishah's. Her confidence in her own character and loyalty, and in her Rabb that she would soon be exonerated, bore its fruits and the Qur'an bears eternal testimony to her uprightness.

It is ʿĀ'ishah ﵂ who narrates to us that the Prophet ﷺ comforted the community of Muslims who had endured boycott, torture and rejection for their proclamations of faith, saying, 'No calamity befalls a Muslim but that Allah expiates some of his/her sins because of it, even if it were [just] the prick of a thorn.'[10] As such, then, when we find ourselves afflicted let us be reminded that perhaps the difficulty we are experiencing holds within it the blessing of expiation for sins we have not had the fortitude to seek repentance for. Or perhaps this calamity holds within it a lesson from which we and those around us may learn and grow. As we are repeatedly told by the Messenger of Allah ﷺ, every affair of the believer is good: when a blessing comes to us, we thank Allah and the rewards we receive increase; when a difficulty comes to us, we are patient and steadfast and then too, our rewards increase.

Do not use Allah as an excuse to refrain from good deeds

> A man came to ʿĀ'ishah ؓ and told her that he had sworn an oath by Allah that he would not speak to a particular individual again, and if he did, he would free all the slaves he had and give away all of his wealth. ʿĀ'ishah ؓ instructed the man to neither emancipate his slaves nor give away his wealth, but to break his oath and pay an expiation for it due to Allah's Words, 'And do not make Allah an excuse against being righteous and fearing Allah and making peace among people. And Allah is All-Hearing, All-Knowing.'[11]

ʿĀ'ishah ؓ knew only too well the context of revelation for this verse from Surah al-Baqarah that she quoted to the Companion. During the intensely harmful period of the slander against her, it was not only ʿĀ'ishah ﷺ who was gripped by the enormity of the lies and gossip that were weaving their way through Madinah, but also her family, particularly her parents. What added to the immensity of their woes was the sting of betrayal when they found out who carried these tales across the city. Madinah, the City of Light, was ambushed by an insurmountable darkness as the rumours against ʿĀ'ishah's fidelity and integrity ravaged the Muslim community and delighted the community of hypocrites and enemies of Islam. Among those engaged in actively spreading those lies was none other than Misṭaḥ ibn Uthāthah, the nephew of Abu Bakr ﷺ.

Misṭaḥ's betrayal was exacerbated by the fact that Abu Bakr ﷺ had taken his nephew under his wing and regularly provided him with financial support. When verses descended on the matter, they absolved ʿĀ'ishah ﷺ of the slander, redeemed her character, elevated her position and forever warned against unfairly and unfoundedly accusing a woman in attempts to defame her. Abu Bakr ﷺ was not only relieved, but his hurt and sense of vindication turned towards Misṭaḥ, leading Abu Bakr ﷺ to swear an oath that he would henceforth withdraw charitable support of his nephew for his unseemly role in spreading the lies about his beloved daughter.

It was upon this severe oath by the normally genteel Abu Bakr ﷺ, that the words of Allah Most High were revealed: *And do not make Allah an excuse against being righteous and fearing Allah and making peace among people. And Allah is All-Hearing, All-Knowing* (al-Baqarah 2: 224). Yes, Abu Bakr ؓ and his family had endured a terrible ordeal, and yes, their family was left on the precipice of disrepute, but had Allah not intervened and restored balance? How many women can claim Divine intervention in their affairs, in a manner that safeguards not only them but all Muslim women thereafter?

Abu Bakr's additional punishment of Misṭaḥ had led to tipping the balance of justice towards the creation of an injustice on two counts—firstly, in depriving an already crestfallen Misṭaḥ and secondly, in Abu Bakr ؓ depriving himself of the rewards of showing magnanimity and in continuing his act of charity towards his own family. It is easy to show magnanimity and generosity to those who benefit from our charity remotely and from afar; the true test of our munificence is in being able to maintain and uphold it with those who are nearest to us, embroiled in our own personal politics and whose negative qualities and characteristics are only too close and too evident to us.

Allah outrightly rejects those actions which lead to hiding behind Him, deeming them as acts that are not done in service of Allah and instead born of the ego and desires of individuals. It is important that we are all vigilant against this. Abu Bakr ؓ was among the senior Companions of the Prophet ﷺ, a beloved friend of his, and one of the earliest Muslims. He believed unfalteringly when the Prophet ﷺ said he had gone on an overnight journey to Jerusalem and back, riding on a creature that resembled a mule and had wings. That was the depth of his faith. Yet even he almost fell foul to the machinations of his lower self while taking an oath in Allah's Name, garbing the ego's desire in a cloak of sanctimony. This verse, and ʿĀ'ishah's safeguarding of the Muslim heart by invoking it, is a reminder for each of us to remain alert to the ways in which we may betray ourselves from doing what is right while still convincing ourselves of our own righteousness by taking Allah's name in order to do so. Allah ﷻ tells us that those who *from their own covetousness are saved—it is they, they that shall attain a happy state* (*al-ḥashr* 59: 9).

Finding strength in the Creator over the Creation

> Muʿāwiyah ؓ wrote to ʿĀ'ishah ؓ, Mother of the Believers, asking her to write back to him with words of advice that would not overburden him. She wrote back to him saying, 'Peace be upon you, as for what you have requested, I heard the Messenger of Allah ﷺ say, "Whoever seeks Allah's Pleasure by incurring the wrath of the people, Allah will suffice for him/her as a support against the people, and whoever seeks the pleasure of the people by incurring the wrath of Allah, then Allah leaves this person to the people."'[12]

ʿĀ'ishah ﵂ was to come to know well the power and redemption to be found in entrusting all of one's affairs to Allah alone when faced by the onslaught of the worst of people's character and behaviour, but she had also spent many years observing the practice of her beloved husband. Having migrated to Madinah and been welcomed with joy and love by its Muslim inhabitants, the early days in Madinah were ones during which the Prophet ﷺ was still haunted by a fear of the Quraysh and the traumas they had inflicted upon him and his community. The reality of safety from their harm had not yet become settled in the mind of the Prophet ﷺ. Additionally, it was not long before the hypocrites and dissenters began to antagonise the Prophet ﷺ in Madinah too by sowing seeds of doubt about his leadership and Prophecy.

ʿĀ'ishah ﵂ commented on this period of his life and reported his feelings of worry that had created in him a defensiveness around people and a need in him to retreat into himself. One night as he prepared to sleep, he confided to ʿĀ'ishah ﵂ that he felt unsafe and wished he could call upon one of his Companions to stand guard over him through the night. Not long had passed before they heard a sound stirring outside their door. The couple called out, 'Who is there?' It was Saʿd ibn Abī Waqqās ﵁, standing with his sword in hand. Saʿd ﵁ said, 'A fear stirred within me about the safety of the Messenger of Allah so I came to stand guard.'

The Prophet ﷺ supplicated to God in favour of Saʿd ؓ and was finally able to sleep. And so, the days and nights passed in anxiety for the safety of the Prophet ﷺ until Allah revealed the words: *O Messenger, announce that which has been revealed upon you from your Rabb, and if you do not do so, then you have not conveyed His Message. And Allah will protect you from the people. Indeed, Allah does not guide the obstinate disbelievers* (*al-Mā'idah* 5: 67). ʿĀ'ishah ؓ reported that when these words of encouragement and promise were revealed, the Prophet ﷺ raised his head out of the window to address his Companions loyally guarding him through the nights, and declared, 'O people! Go, for Allah will protect me!'[13]

The previous reminder calls for us to undertake introspection and safeguard our deeds from the intrusions of the ego, it reminds us that if we stay true to our covenant with Allah as believers, then Allah will suffice for us in all our affairs, particularly in protecting us from those who would seek to do us harm for our commitment to Allah. In this statement, we are reminded that if we take account of ourselves regularly and return to purifying our intentions and actions daily, we can also have confidence that Allah will protect us from the people, whoever they may be and whatever powers they may wield. Whether it is in family hierarchies or the politics of the world we live in, Muslims must assert themselves in establishing justice and Allah's sovereignty on Earth by speaking against the tyrannical with truth, by exercising patience in the process of affecting change, and by standing with the weak and oppressed.

The importance of the pursuit of justice in the life of Muslims

Regarding the verse of the Qur'an wherein Allah ﷻ says: *And We shall set up the Balances of Justice on the Day of Resurrection (al-Baqarah 21: 47)*, Imam al-Ṭabarī relays a story about ʿĀʾishah ﵂:

> A man came and sat in front of the Messenger of Allah ﷺ and told him about two slaves he had who were recalcitrant so he would beat them. In response to this man's statement, ʿĀʾishah ﵂ said that the Prophet ﷺ replied, 'The extent to which they betrayed, disobeyed and lied to you, will be measured against your punishment of them. If your punishment is greater than their misdeeds, then some of your rewards will be taken from you and given to them.' The man began to weep upon hearing the words of the Messenger of Allah ﷺ, who in turn told him, 'You should read what Allah has said in His Book,' and he recited the aforementioned verse. The man then declared, 'By Allah, O Messenger of Allah, I see nothing better for myself than to part from them. Bear witness that they are both free.'[14]

Though not one of her own statements, ʿĀʾishah ‎ relays a key learning point for the astute Muslim in this exchange. The Prophet ﷺ is presented with this predicament by a believer complaining as a master about his slaves, and while society had set up, and continues to set up, unfair and unjust hierarchies, the Prophet ﷺ himself does not justify these hierarchies nor does his response acknowledge them. Both the misdeeds of the master—his verbal and physical abuse of the slaves—and those of the slaves—their betrayal, lying and deception—would be measured against one another with equitable strength when the Balance is set on the Day of Resurrection. Moreover, the Prophet ﷺ does not mention the possibility of the slaves' misdeeds outweighing those of the master; he only mentions the eventuality of the master's misdeeds outweighing those of the slaves—an acute recognition of the power dynamic between them.

In a society that had constructed unjust hierarchies and structures that oppressed people designated as slaves, the Prophet ﷺ is acknowledging that the man is far more likely to transgress against them than they are likely or even able to transgress against him. In turn, this man, a true believer, recognised instantly the severity of what was before him. Were the privileges he had and the oppressive power structures that had delivered slaves to him worth standing in fear and humiliation on the Day of Resurrection? Would the feeling of power, strength, and dominion over the weak, feeble, and marginalised be worth witnessing the scales of justice tipping against him when his deeds were taken to account? Surely the answer was no every time, and he professed immediately that he had set his slaves free, thereby simultaneously setting his own soul free from the worst outcome in the next life.

A similar recognition is found in the assertion of Allah regarding orphan girls. It is recorded in al-Bukhārī that ʿĀ'ishah ﵁ was asked by ʿUrwah ibn Zubayr ﵀ regarding the verse: *If you fear that you shall not be able to deal justly with the orphan girls* (*al-Nisā'* 4: 3). She informed him:

> O nephew, there was an orphan girl who was under the care of a man whose wealth she would share in [as his ward] and he was attracted to both her wealth [which he did not have access to] and her beauty, so he intended to marry her at a much lower *ṣidāq*[15] than what someone else would have gifted her. So, such guardians were forbidden from marrying them unless they would do justice by their wards by gifting them the highest *ṣidāq* of what another suitor would have bestowed upon them. Otherwise, they were ordered to marry other women of their choice rather than those orphan girls.
>
> They were forbidden from marrying those orphan girls whose wealth and beauty they desired, unless [those men] did so with justice,

> and that was because they would refrain from marrying these orphan girls if they were lacking in property and beauty.[16]

Once more the Words of Allah address the social injustices created by people, in this case the weak position afforded to women and girls, particularly orphan girls. Later in the same chapter of the Qur'an, Allah declares: *O you who have believed, be persistently standing firm in justice, witnesses for Allah, even if it be against yourselves or parents and relatives. Whether one is rich or poor, Allah is more worthy of both* (*al-Nisā'* 4: 135). As Muslims we should seek out justice in our every action, from the serving of food to our children, to our dealings with our staff or colleagues, to the way we exercise our rights, and to the way we fulfil our civic, social and familial duties, all should be carried out with an integrity that is rooted in speaking the truth and enacting justice, mindful that as Muslims it is our purpose to right the imbalance of injustices in this world, even and especially if this means surrendering our own privileges, so that in the next life the Balance of our deeds is tipped in our favour.

Supplicating to Allah to keep our hearts firm upon faith

In Surah *Āl ʿImrān*, verse 7, Allah refers to the *ūlul-albāb*, people of understanding, whom He defines in the next verse as those who say: *Our Rabb, do not deviate our hearts after you have guided it. Grant us your Mercy, indeed You are the Bestower* (*Āl ʿImrān* 3: 8).

Ibn Kathīr, in his *tafsīr* of this verse, states that ʿĀ'ishah ﵂ reported:

> The Prophet's most oft-repeated supplication was 'O Turner of hearts, keep my heart firm upon Your Way (يا مقلب القلوب ثبت قلبي على دينك).' ʿĀ'ishah ﵂ asked why he was so committed to this *duʿā*'. The Prophet ﷺ replied, 'There is no heart except that it is poised between the two fingers of the Most Merciful. If He wishes He may keep it established upon uprightness, and if He wishes He may cause it to deviate.'

The importance of this *duʿā*' cannot be overstated. The previous three statements have expounded on the importance of sincerity and the pursuit of justice in the life of a Muslim and to do so with absolute reliance upon Allah. For a believer to be able to exert themselves in any of these endeavours, it is important that the heart, the seat of sincerity and integrity, is sound and firm in its submission to Allah, for it is the guiding compass by which a Muslim navigates this life, and it is all that we will stand before Allah with on the Day of Judgement. Neither children nor spouses, not status nor wealth, not education nor caste nor social status will avail us on the Day that the Scales are raised. It is as Allah ﷻ tells us: *The Day when neither wealth nor children will avail, except one who brings to Allah a truthful and secure heart* (*al-Shuʿarā'* 26: 88-89).

Prophetic guidance informs us of the many ways in which we can purify our hearts. The Prophet ﷺ not only held on fastidiously to this supplication as witnessed and remarked upon by ʿĀ'ishah ؓ but also gave his community other actions through which to keep the heart sound and firm. These include clearing one's heart of any resentment or ill feeling towards a fellow believer and to ensure that they are safe from our tongues and our actions, to fast regularly, to give in charity, to show kindness to orphans and others in need, to regularly turn to Allah in repentance, to make much remembrance of Allah, to exhibit a generosity and kindness of character, to abstain from sin, and to invest in periods of meditative silences ... to name but a few. To fortify the efforts of the limbs are the affirmations of the tongue, and there is no better affirmation than this *duʿā'*.

Fiqh of ʿĀʾishah

*T*his section discusses some of ʿĀʾishah's jurisprudential positions. These are offered as an illustration of her consideration and understanding of some of the practicalities of being a Muslim woman seeking to live according to the precepts of Islam. Some of the positions run counter to dominant *fiqh* positions, and the reader is advised to research and consult authorities whom they trust in order to come to their own conclusions. I also refer the reader back to the introductory comments of the previous chapter on ʿĀʾishah's contributions to the *tafsīr* tradition.

Nonetheless, the status of ʿĀʾishah ﷺ in matters of jurisprudence is unrivalled. The famous fifteenth-century scholar Ibn Ḥajar al-ʿAsqalānī wrote that 'one-quarter of the laws of Shariah are based on the [the traditions of] ʿĀʾishah,' a formidable feat for any Companion of the Prophet ﷺ, and indicative of the mastery she had over the various facets of Islamic knowledge production in line with the objectives of Allah, the mission of the Prophet ﷺ and the eternal trajectory of the Qur'an in setting Muslims on an ascending path to the *tawḥīdic* vision.

Women's Travel

> It is recorded that ʿĀ'ishah ﵂ was informed that Abū Saʿīd al-Khuḍri ﵁ was claiming that the Messenger of Allah ﷺ had forbidden women from traveling unless accompanied by a *maḥram*. The narrator, ʿAmrah ﵂ said, "ʿĀ'ishah ﵂ then turned to the womenfolk in her company and said, "Not all of you has a *maḥram*.""[17]

A similar tradition is also reported by Ibn Abī Shaybah, and again he too reports ʿĀ'ishah's response as being, 'not all women have a *maḥram*.' Some scholars have chosen to read ʿĀ'ishah's response as an affirming of the apparent prohibition of the Prophet ﷺ on women travelling alone, while others have said that she was bringing to attention the inconvenience such a stance creates and the impracticality of it especially in the lives of Muslim women who do not have any *maḥram* who could escort them on their travels. Indeed, there are women who do have *maḥram*, but cannot rely on them to be available for every journey they wish to make. It is most likely that she was in fact of the latter belief, having herself travelled from Madinah to Makkah to perform the hajj after the death of the Prophet ﷺ without a *maḥram*.

We know that the Prophet ﷺ asserted that a time of such safety would come when women would 'travel from Ḥīrah [Iraq] to circumambulate the Kaaba fearing none but Allah.'[18] It could be argued that the original prohibition of the Prophet ﷺ that Abū Saʿīd al-Khuḍri ؓ was repeating was contingent on the context in which the Prophet ﷺ was speaking, at a time when Muslims were few in number, did not hold any sort of power and could not extend any security. By the time Umar ibn al-Khaṭṭāb ؓ was Caliph, not only had the Muslim empire expanded extensively, but Muslims were also many in number and a far cry from the humble and vulnerable beginnings when the Prophet ﷺ had forbidden independent travel for Muslim women out of fear and concern for their safety. As a result, it is under the Caliphate of Umar ibn al-Khaṭṭāb ؓ that ʿĀ'ishah ؓ set out on her pilgrimage to Makkah without a *maḥram*, even when she had *maḥrams* available to her.

On the need to unravel braids for *ghusl*

It is reported by Muslim that it was brought to ʿĀ'ishah's attention that:

> Ibn ʿAmr ؓ had instructed women to undo their braids when they perform their *ghusl*. ʿĀ'ishah ؓ remarked, 'How strange is Ibn

> ʿAmr's instruction! He orders the women to undo their braids when doing their *ghusl*! Why doesn't he just order them to shave their heads? The Messenger of Allah ﷺ and I used to bathe from the same vessel, and I would not exceed pouring it over my head three times.'[19]

Al-Nasā'ī records this same ḥadith but adds that ʿĀ'ishah said, 'and I did not undo my hair.'

For many Muslim women, and indeed men too, for whom locks, dreads or braids are the most natural, protective, and convenient way to keep their hair, the demand for hair to be undone in order to perform *ghusl* imposes a significant burden. ʿĀ'ishah's opposition to this demand is also corroborated by the position of Umm Salamah who is recorded by Muslim as having asked the Prophet ﷺ, 'Messenger of Allah, I am a woman with many braids, do I need to undo them for the purification bath after menses?' The Prophet ﷺ responded, 'No, it is sufficient that you sprinkle water over your head three times, and the water will do in purifying you.'[20]

The *ghusl* is a performative marker of the exit of a believer from a state of metaphysical impurity and entry into a metaphysical state of purity. There is often little actual impurity on the body, and certainly none in the hair that requires such absolute drenching of the head. As such then the Prophet ﷺ was lenient and inclusive in his praxis and instruction regarding braids and ghusl.[21]

On perfume while in a state of *Iḥrām*

Al-Bukhārī and Muslim record on the authority of Ibrāhīm ibn Muhammad ibn al-Muntashir, on the authority of his father who said:

> I heard Ibn ʿUmar ﷺ saying, 'That I should be daubed with a trickle of water is preferable to me than to be a *muḥrim* doused in perfume.' Then I entered upon ʿĀ'ishah ﷺ and informed her of what Ibn ʿUmar ﷺ had said. She responded, 'I perfumed the Messenger of Allah, and he would visit his wives, and he would then enter into *iḥrām*.'

Whilst it is an established and accepted condition for the one in *iḥrām* to abstain from using perfume, ʿĀ'ishah ﷺ makes it clear that Prophetic practice allowed for perfume to be applied to clothing before formally entering into the state of *iḥrām*. Interestingly, al-Bayhaqī records in his *Sunan* that Ibn ʿUmar ﷺ said, 'I heard ʿUmar say, "When you have done the stoning and shaved [your heads] then everything is permissible for you except women and perfume."' Sālim ﷺ said that ʿĀ'ishah ﷺ said, 'Everything except women. I perfumed the Messenger of Allah ﷺ as he came out of the state of ritual consecration (*taḥlīl*).'

Whilst ʿĀ'ishah ﷺ may have enjoyed perfumes simply for the love of their scent, there is even in this instruction a spiritual lesson to be taken for those who will take the time to ponder it. ʿĀ'ishah ﷺ does not undermine the stipulation that the *muḥrim* is to not apply perfume or use perfumed products, rather she is safeguarding against an excessive attitude towards religious rites and rituals, which, if one becomes too prescriptive in regarding, can become a distraction from the spiritual activity at hand. How often have we witnessed in our community the disruption, turmoil and disunity caused by differences over technical issues pertaining to ritualistic elements of Islam, to the detriment of both our connections with Allah and one another?

By considering deeply ʿĀʾishah's response to the issue of perfume for the *muḥrim*, one is invited to remain focused on the purpose of the ritual rather than its technicalities; to see Allah and a path to all those actions beloved to Him, rather than to be distracted by the details and remain stuck on those, for that would be a terrible loss and paltry exchange.

When a woman starts her period while she is performing the Hajj

Ibn ʿAbbās and Zayd ibn Thābit ☙ disagreed on the ruling regarding a woman who has per-formed the requisite circumambulation of the Kaaba (*ṭawāf*) on the third day of hajj (*Yawm al-Naḥr*) who then experiences the beginning of her menses. Zayd ☙ said, 'She should stay in her home until her menses is complete.' Ibn ʿAbbās ☙, however said, 'She should hurry to perform her *ṭawāf* on *Yawm al-Naḥr*.' The Anṣār present said, 'O Ibn ʿAbbās, if you continue to conflict with Zayd, we will not follow you.' Ibn ʿAbbās ﷺ responded, 'Ok, go and ask your companion on the matter, Umm Salīm.' So, they went and questioned her, and she informed them of what had happened to Ṣafiyyah bint Ḥuyyay ﷺ. She reported that ʿĀ'ishah ﷺ said, 'Safiyyah bint Huyyay came on her period [whilst on hajj], so she mentioned this to the Prophet ﷺ, and he ordered to her to be hasty.'[22]

As has been noted by other scholars,[23] pre-Islamic attitude was thoroughly phobic and hostile towards women's menstruation. Instead of being viewed as part of the life-producing biological system that Allah has created in women, it was regarded as a source of both spiritual and physical impurity, with women having to endure all manner of difficulty on top of their periods each month. Islam and the message with which the Prophet ﷺ was sent was radical in so many ways, not least in its rejection of this ignorant practice and attitude. This meant that a woman, when she was on her period was not to be exited from her room or bed, that she was not deemed physically impure, nor inherently defiled. Instead, she was welcomed to rest, with Allah Most Generous and Kind even permitting an amnesty for women each month from their duty to establish their prayers and fasting in the month of Ramadan. For most women, this is a welcome respite during their periods; however on the issue of hajj, a period could cause much disappointment and disruption. In a time when medications are now available to delay the onset of a period and can usually be easily arranged for women planning travel to perform the hajj, perhaps the enormity of the Prophet's response is not fully appreciated. For many people hajj is still a once in a lifetime opportunity, were a woman to find her efforts in preparing for and saving up to go on hajj, and in almost completing all its rites come to naught because of her period, a biological function outside of her control, would be devastating.

The status of a child born out of wedlock

Al-ḥākim records in his *Mustadrak*, in the chapter on 'Freeing Slaves', that ʿUrwah said:

> It reached ʿĀ'ishah ﵂ that Abū Hurayrah ﵁ said that the Messenger of Allah ﷺ had said, 'That I should give a whip in the Path of Allah is more beloved to me than to free the child [born] of adultery,' and that he [also] said, 'The child [born] of adultery is the worst of

[the] three.'[24]...ʿĀ'ishah ﷺ responded, 'May Allah have mercy on Abū Hurayrah! He listened poorly and thus explained poorly. As for his saying, "That I should give a whip in the Path of Allah, is more beloved to me than to free the child [born] of adultery," this was because when the verses, *But he would not try to ascend the steep uphill path. And what could make you conceive what that steep uphill path is? It is the freeing of a neck [from the bondage of slavery* (*al-Balad* 90: 11–13), were revealed, it was said to the Messenger of Allah ﷺ, "We do not have one that we could emancipate, but one of us has a Black slave girl who serves him. If we order them to fornicate, then they will bear us children whom we could then emancipate." The Messenger of Allah ﷺ then said, "That I should give a whip in the Path of Allah, is more beloved to me than to free the child [born] of adultery." As for his saying, "The child [born] of adultery is the worst of [the] three," there is no such statement of the Messenger ﷺ. Actually, a man from among the hypocrites was troubling the Messenger of Allah ﷺ, so he said, "Who will relieve me of [this man]?" It was [then] said, "O Messenger of Allah, among his other [blameworthy traits] is that he is a child of adultery," to which the Messenger of Allah ﷺ replied, "He is worst of the three," and Allah Most High stated,

"No bearer of burdens shall be made to bear another's burden."'[25]

This intervention by ʿĀʾishah ❦ seeks to destigmatise the child born of an adulterous relationship, whilst not reducing the severity of the offence committed by the parents. In pre-Islamic Arabia it was commonplace for a child to be charged for the crimes of its parents. For example, a father who had committed the crime of murder could have his son substitute him for retribution. When Islam was revealed to the Prophet ❦, many unjust practices were challenged and rebuked, and this was one such practice refuted by Allah. Sins and crimes belong only to the individual who committed the crime and cannot be inherited by or transferred to their offspring.

In another tradition recorded by Muslim, it is noted that ʿĀʾishah ❦ was asked whether or not a person who was born out of wedlock could perform the duty of imam and lead a Muslim congregation in prayer. She responded by saying, 'There is nothing from the sin of his parents upon him,' and then proceeded to quote the Qurʾan: *No soul shall bear the burdens of another* (al-Anʿām 6: 164), and *the most honoured of you in the Sight of Allah, is the one with most taqwā* (al-ḥujurāt 49:13). She also cited the Prophet ❦ as saying: 'The one who recites [the Qurʾan] best from amongst you should lead the prayer, and if they are all equal in recitation, then the one best in manners, and if they are all equal in their manners, then the one who is eldest in age.'[26]

Neither Allah, the Prophet ﷺ nor his beloved wife, ʿĀ'ishah ﵂, condone the practice of burdening a child, or any other person in proximity of a sin, with taking responsibility for that sin. While nowadays no one seeks to substitute a child for its parent's position when it comes to meting out punishments for a crime, the attitude remains and manifests itself in other ways. How often in some Muslim societies is a person denied an opportunity due to the misgivings of their parents? Or how often is an entirely human-made caste system in which people are marked out as superior or inferior based on what caste they were born into, invoked to prevent an individual from succeeding? Marriages, education, job opportunities and more are often denied in a manner that can only feel punitive to the person or people on the receiving end of such behaviour, for a reason that has nothing to do with anything that person has any control over, and which is not validated by Allah.

On the need to perform wuḍū' after performing *ghusl* on the deceased

It is reported on the authority of Yaḥya ibn ʿAbd al-Raḥmān ibn Hatib ﵁ who narrated that:

> Abū Hurayrah ﵁ said, 'Whoever performs the *ghusl*, ritual washing of the deceased, must also perform the *ghusl*, and whoever touched

> it must perform ablution (*wuḍūʾ*).' When this reached ʿĀʾishah ﷺ, she remarked, 'Have the deceased of the Muslims become impure? And what of a man who has carried the body?'[27]

There are refutations of this statement by Abū Hurayrah ﷺ by Companions such as Ibn Masʿūd ﷺ and others, but ʿĀʾishah's correction is not only instructive in terms of the jurisprudential issue being raised, but also in the type of pedagogy she is embodying. Rather than responding as Ibn Masʿūd ﷺ did, who said, 'O people, you are not made impure by your dead,' ʿĀʾishah ﷺ engages what would now be described as Socratic questioning. Rather than refuting Abū Huraryah ﷺ outright, ʿĀʾishah ﷺ engages him and the Muslims as an audience by inviting them to think logically about what is implied by such a position if it were to be accepted. She asks, 'Have the deceased of the Muslims become impure?' thereby pushing for contemplation on *why* this would be so, and on the basis of *what* could this be accepted.

She astutely skips the issue of those who washed the body and asks, '…and what of a man who has carried the body?' At this point there has been no mention of the one who has carried the body, only the one who has washed it, but by extending the question to the next person in the chain of those who service the deceased, she is both practising and demonstrating how to develop critical thinking.

If the deceased is now impure, and those who have washed the body also suffer impurity, then what of the next person in the process of the *janāzah*? What are the limits and parameters of this impurity? What is its nature and how far reaching is it?

It is well established that Allah demands of His believers that they engage the critical faculties they have been blessed with, often asking all people to look around and bear witness to Allah's creation and magnificence and to contemplate it deeply. In responding to an inaccurate portrayal of the Sunnah by provoking a question, ʿĀ'ishah ﵂ is safeguarding and ensuring that practice of thinking as ordained and commanded by Allah for the believers of a religion that did away with middlemen and clergy. She can be seen to do so in other traditions too, as has been relayed in her response to Ibn ʿAmr ﵁ and his assertion that Muslim women need to undo their braids to perform *ghusl* and in her response to Abū Saʿīd al-Khuḍri ﵁ and his assertion that women cannot travel without a male guardian. She does not always simply offer an answer, because the astute teacher knows that the greatest gift they can give to their student is not the answer, but the means to arriving at the answer. The means by which ʿĀ'ishah ﵂ arrives at her conclusions is her intelligence, guided by her *taqwā*, which is guided by what she witnessed of the Prophet ﷺ, and ultimately by what is clearly expressed in the Guidance of Allah's Words in the Qur'an.

Whether a woman nullifies the prayer

> It reached ʿĀ'ishah ﵂ that Abū Hurayrah ﵁ said, 'A woman nullifies the prayer [if she walks in front of a person offering the prayer].' So, she said, 'The Messenger of Allah ﷺ would pray and tuck my feet between his hands or his thighs. Then he would push them back [when prostrating], and I would stretch them forward [when he would raise his head from prostration].'[28]

In a narration of a similar ḥadith recorded by Aḥmad it is menstruating women who are specified, a stigmatisation of menses that we have already seen is rooted in pre-Islamic Jāhiliyyah and one of the many ignorant practices the Prophet ﷺ was to oppose in his life and praxis. Muslim and al-Bukhārī narrate similar traditions in which ʿĀ'ishah ﵂ is informed that not only has it been stated that a woman's passing in front of one who is in prayer nullifies the prayer, but that 'woman' is one in that category alongside dogs and donkeys too. Contrastingly, al-Bukhārī also records that in response to this, ʿĀ'ishah ﵂ asks, 'Do you make us like donkeys and dogs?' before describing how the Prophet ﷺ prayed with her feet tucked between his hands or thighs.[29]

Many scholars, both classical and contemporary have sought to tackle the problematic notion that a woman could nullify the prayer. Imam al-Nawawī insisted that what is meant is not that the prayer is annulled but that it is disrupted as the woman is distracting for the male worshipper. Others have less imaginatively argued that there is nothing wrong with being classified alongside dogs and donkeys, for we are all Allah's creations.

ʿĀ'ishah's intervention does away with any need for linguistic analysis or philosophising on the nature of Allah's creation. From this intimate picture depicted by this beloved wife of the Prophet ﷺ, we not only benefit from the rejection of classifying women among dogs and donkeys as nullifiers of the prayer, but we are also nurtured by the vision of a prayerful pious man, who lived in humble settings, limited in the space around him whilst in prayer, but remaining simultaneously a loving and caring husband. In such a small space, he could have made his wife feel unimportant, a distraction from God, asked her to sit behind or away from him, or maybe even to leave the room, but he did not. The Prophet ﷺ was a man whose heart was vast; with a space for his Lord that no one could intrude upon and a space for his wife, carefully carved out and preserved.

On *Ṣalāt al-Ḍuḥā*

> It is recorded by al-Bukhārī that ʿĀ'ishah ؓ was asked about the supererogatory prayer, *ṣalāt al-Ḍuḥā*. She said, 'I did not see the Prophet ﷺ perform *ṣalāt al-Ḍuḥā*, but I do

pray it. And there is nothing more beloved to me than that the people pray its two units too.'[30]

To the untrained eye this statement may at first seem contradictory. If ʿĀʾishah 🙏 had not seen the Prophet 🙏 praying this voluntary prayer, then why does she perform it and why does she love to see the community engage in it? Imam al-Bayhaqī has explained that ʿĀʾishah 🙏 has employed a rhetorical device to emphasize how rarely the Prophet 🙏 prayed this prayer. Implicit in her statement is that he prayed it so rarely, it is almost as if he never did, but it is a prayer she loves so it was one that she does not abandon. In fact, in a similar tradition recorded by Muslim, it is stated that her response to ʿAbdullāh ibn Shaqīq 🙏, when he enquired as to whether the Prophet 🙏 prayed ṣalāt al-Ḍuḥā, was to say, 'No, except for when he returned from his travels.'

ʿĀʾishah's intervention and practice illustrates that the voluntary supererogatory prayers of the Prophet 🙏 can be followed and adapted in a manner that does not contradict the bounds of Islam but that deliver the greatest spiritual return to the believer. For the Prophet 🙏, ṣalāt al-Ḍuḥā was a prayer performed in gratitude upon his safe return from a journey. For ʿĀʾishah 🙏, it became a daily practice of communing with Allah.

Allah says in the Qur'an: *Indeed this is a Reminder, so let, whosoever wills, to take a path (sabīlun) to their Lord* (*al-Insān* 76: 29). How fascinating that Allah says, 'a path' and not 'the Path'. The way to Allah is the Straight Path, but for that, Allah uses a term we are all familiar with from Surah al-Fatihah, *al-ṣirāṭ al-Mustaqīm*; so what then of this indefinite path to Allah? Perhaps it is better to think of this latter undefined path as a lane that one takes up on the Straight Path to Allah. To think of the Straight Path to Allah as submission to Allah, and the undefined path (*sabīlun),* as the path we ourselves forge in our attempt to traverse this journey to Allah. We all have our own strengths and possibilities, for some that may be in prayer, for others it may be fasting, giving in charity, showing kindness to others, engaging in *dhikr*, and for others yet it may be in pursuing knowledge, educating, community building and so on and so forth—the list is endless.

What is important is that each of us in our engaged surrender to Allah create for ourselves a unique path to Him built of sincere actions and a desire to meet Him, pleasing and well-pleased.[31] Each day let us ask ourselves which lane we will take on the Path to Allah; which range of deeds will we commit to in our journey back to Allah? Let us be guided by the wisdom of the Messenger of Allah ﷺ who advised, 'The most beloved deeds to Allah are those which are performed consistently, even if they are small.'[32] For nothing is too small in the Sight of Allah, and Allah's generosity will never be exhausted by the good in which we exert ourselves.

On when to break fast

> Two men came to ʿĀʾishah ❧ and said to her,
> 'Mother of the Believers, there are two men
> from the Companions of Muhammad ﷺ; one
> of whom hastens to break his fast and to pray
> and the second who delays breaking the fast
> and praying.' She asked, 'Who is the one that
> hastens breaking his fast and praying?' They
> informed her it was ʿAbdullāh ibn Masʿūd ❧,
> to which she replied: 'That is the way of the
> Messenger of Allah ﷺ.'[33]

Islam is ease and creates ease.[34] The days of fasting are made easier by the believer's contentment
in the knowledge that they are pleasing their Lord.
The heart is filled by the glad tidings of the rewards
that await the fasting believer in this life and the
next, and so the stomach follows the heart even if
begrudgingly, at times. As for the time of breaking
fast, then the Sunnah of the Prophet ﷺ was to petition Allah to grant ease for his community, and the
Sunnah of Allah was in responding and delivering
ease to the *ummah* of Muhammad ﷺ. The breaking
of the fast promptly is from the blessings and mer-
cies of Allah, and from the perfectly balanced way
of Islam. Allah urges us in in the Qur'an saying, *Seek
the home of the Hereafter by that which Allah has
given you, but do not forget your share of the world*
(*al-Qaṣaṣ* 28: 77). In other words, dedicate yourself

in engaged surrender to Allah, in what Islam has guided you to by seeking out acts of worship to occupy yourself with, but do not overextend yourself, and take from the bounties, blessings and gifts that Allah has bestowed on you in the form of this life and the permissible worldly joys it contains.

On ostentatious living

Zayd ibn Khālid ﷺ said that he heard Abū Ṭalḥah ﷺ state that he had heard:

> The Messenger of Allah ﷺ said, 'Angels do not enter a house in which there is a dog nor if there is a statue.' Zayd ibn Khālid replied, 'Let's go to ʿĀ'ishah and ask her regarding this.' He went to her and Zayd ibn Khālid addressed her saying, 'O Mother, he [Abū Ṭalḥa] has informed me that the Prophet ﷺ said, "Angels do not enter a house in which there is a dog nor if there is a statue." Did you hear the Messenger of Allah ﷺ mentioning this?' She replied, 'No, but I will inform you of what I witnessed him do. He had gone out on an expedition, and I was awaiting his caravan, so I took a throw and used it as a curtain. When he arrived, I welcomed him at the door saying, "May the Peace and Mercy of Allah be upon you Messenger of Allah, all praise be to Allah who has honoured you, given you victory and elevated you." He looked about the house

and saw the curtain. He did not say anything to me, but I could see disapproval in his face. He then came to the curtain and pulled it down saying, "Allah has not commanded us to clothe stones and clay out of the sustenance He has given us." I then cut it to pieces and made two pillows out of it stuffing them with palm fibre, and he did not disapprove of it.'[35]

There are other traditions involving Maymūnah ﵂, another of the Prophet's wives, who had put up a curtain using cloth that had artwork depicting animals on it which she was instructed by the Prophet ﷺ to remove due to the images upon it. Other ḥadith suggest that the presence of a dog in the home is forbidden, though of course this is a matter upon which some jurists have differed, most famously Imam Mālik.[36] But the tradition which ʿĀ'ishah ﵂ relays here is neither concerned with dogs nor images on a cloth. It is unknown what the design of the throw she used as a curtain was, it is plausible that there were some images on the curtain, given the nature of the question that had been posed to ʿĀ'ishah ﵂ by Zayd and Abū Ṭalḥa ﵄, but again, in neither her recounting of the incident nor in the explanation of the Prophet ﷺ is that mentioned. Rather, the Prophet ﷺ stated that the sustenance Allah provides is not for the 'dressing up of stone and clay'.

This is not to say that home furnishings are not allowed, of course curtains were used to separate spaces and provide privacy. Rather, the warning in this instance is that one should not digress into the realm of ostentation as a means of protecting the heart from attachment to this ephemeral world which the Muslim is advised to treat as part of the journey, knowing that the true destination is the afterlife with Allah.

The Prophet 🕮 had friends and beloved Companions who were wealthy and whose displays of wealth did not bother him and regarding which he did not intervene. But for his own family, the Prophet 🕮 preferred simplicity. He wished for his and his family's wealth to be used in the service of his community. He recommended to his own daughter, Fatima 🕮, to replace her gold bangles with steel ones dyed with saffron, and he dissuaded her from taking a slave to help her with her housework. He also loved her more than any father has loved a daughter, but in his apparent depriving of her, he was in fact doing what he believed would save her heart from attachment to a world that is illusory in order to fix it on one that is permanent. Even as a prophet, he was offered by Jibrāʾīl 🕮 that he could be made a Prophet King like Sulaymān 🕮 or a Prophet Servant, humble and modest in his living. The Prophet 🕮 repeatedly stated, 'No, but for me is to be a Prophet Servant.'[37]

Whilst there is nothing wrong with amassing wealth and enjoying the blessings of Allah upon us, it is important for our hearts and souls to reflect on the commitment of the Prophet ﷺ to a modest life, to reminds ourselves of what is important in the bigger picture, in aiding us to divest of capitalism's relentless push to drive us further and further into the rat race of gathering wealth that benefits no one and has no purpose beyond ostentation; the race that degrades us so terribly that once removed at the end of life reveals that no humans remain, only rats.

3

ʿĀ'ishah رضي الله عنها on Matters of ʿAqīdah

This chapter provides an insight into ʿĀ'ishah's stance on several issues pertaining to ʿaqīdah, or theological/creedal positions in Islam.

Al-Bukhārī and Muslim both record in their respective *ṣiḥāḥ*, that ʿAmr ibn al-ʿāṣ ﷺ narrates that he had been selected by the Prophet ﷺ as the commander of his army being deployed to Dhāt al-Salāsil. Feeling encouraged by this show of favour from the Prophet ﷺ, ʿAmr ﷺ decided to ask the Prophet ﷺ who was his dearest Companion. The Prophet ﷺ replied, "ʿĀ'ishah.' Unsatisfied with this answer, ʿAmr ﷺ clarified he meant from amongst the men. The Prophet ﷺ said, 'Her father.' Ibn ḥazm stated in his *al-Aḥkām fī Uṣūl al-Aḥkām*, that this hadith was evidence that the Prophet ﷺ had preferred ʿĀ'ishah ؓ above all his other Companions and family members, even above Fatima ؓ, his daughter whom he was known to love with great intensity. As a result, he argued, ʿĀ'ishah ؓ should be given preference in all our affairs in keeping with the Sunnah of the Prophet ﷺ. Truly to do so is to be on a path of truth, intelligence, righteousness, and loyalty to both the words of the Qur'an and the Prophet ﷺ.

Women as a source of bad luck

It is reported that Abū Hurayrah ؓ said: The Messenger of Allah ﷺ said, 'Bad luck is found in three things: the house, the woman, and the horse.' ʿĀ'ishah ؓ responded:

> Abū Hurayrah has not remembered. He entered upon the Messenger of Allah ﷺ as he was saying, 'May Allah curse the Jews [for] saying, bad luck is found in three things: the house, the woman, and the horse.' He heard the last part of the statement but not the first.[38]

In another version of this hadith, recorded by Aḥmad, ʿĀ'ishah ؓ is reported to have been enraged upon hearing this statement being attributed to the honourable Prophet ﷺ, and responded saying, 'By the One who revealed the Qur'an upon Abū al-Qāsim, he never said such a thing, but rather the Prophet of

Allah ﷺ would say, "The people of ignorance used to say, calamity lies in the woman, riding beast, and home."[39] Then she recited: *No calamity can ever befall the earth, and neither your own selves, unless it be [laid down] in Our decree before We bring it into being; verily, all this is easy for God* (*al-ḥadīd* 57: 22).'[40]

ʿĀ'ishah ﷺ contests the incomplete narration being attributed to the Prophet ﷺ, and uses not only knowledge of the context in which he spoke those words, but also the logical evaluation of how the incomplete statement does not cohere with the Qur'anic injunction of Allah's absolute power over all things, because to hold a superstitious belief in the ability of people, objects or animals to so negatively influence a person's destiny is to undermine the totality of Allah's power and control over all things. It is to ascribe partners to Allah by causing people to be fearful and superstitious of women, houses, and horses as if they have some sway over the course of their destinies in a way that only Allah has.

It is also in stark contradiction to many other statements made by the Prophet ﷺ whereby he forbade the community of believers from maintaining pre-Islamic superstitious beliefs, particularly in holding beliefs about bad omens. It furthermore contradicts the Prophetic mindset of optimism and to have a positive interpretation of all that Allah sends our way. The Prophet Muhammad ﷺ famously exclaimed, 'Amazing is the affair of the believer, verily all his affairs are good, and this is for no one except the believer. If some good befalls him, he is grateful and that is good for him. If some harm befalls him, he is patient and that is good for him.'⁴¹ That being the case, then nothing—no house, no woman, no horse—could be viewed as a source of bad luck.

The Muslim is one whose heart is forever connected to Allah, alert to the knowledge that everything that comes their way comes from a Lord that only wants good for those who have submitted to Him, and that all power is in the Hands of the One whom the believer can commune with through *duʿāʾ*, to ask for the good of all things, and seek protection in this same Divine source, from the evil of all things.

Punishment of the believers in the Hereafter

> ʿAlqamah said: 'It was said to ʿĀʾishah ❀ that Abū Hurayrah ❀ narrates the Prophet ﷺ [as saying], "A woman was punished because of her [treatment of] a cat." ʿĀʾishah replied, "The woman was a disbeliever."'⁴²

In another sound narration recorded by Abū Dāwūd it is stated on the authority of ʿAlqamah, 'We were with ʿĀʾishah when Abū Hurayrah entered. She asked, "Are you the one who narrated this report? 'A woman entered the fire of Hell because of a cat she had tied up and did not feed, nor did she give it water.'" Abū Hurayrah replied, "I heard it from the Prophet ﷺ." ʿĀ'ishah said, "Do you know who this woman was? The woman, regardless of what she did, was a disbeliever and the believer is more honoured in the Sight of Allah than that He punish him or her regarding a cat, so when you narrate from the Prophet ﷺ ponder and think carefully of how you narrate."'[43]

The hadith as relayed by Abū Hurayrah, without ʿĀ'ishah's intervention is well-known and oft-repeated, regularly used to illustrate the gentleness advocated by Islam and the broadening of tenderness that is extended beyond humanity to all of God's creation, but ʿĀ'ishah's intervention once again is priceless and its lesson profound.

ʿĀ'ishah reasserts Qur'anic ideals; that people are not to be judged by a singular deed and that which is outwardly apparent is not always an accurate measure of the inward spiritual state of an individual. The entire story of Khiḍr and Mūsā in Surah al-Kahf is designed to impart this wisdom to Muslims.[44] Many a behaviour enacted by Khiḍr appeared abhorrent to Mūsā, and yet behind each one was a grace ordained by Allah. This is not to say that ʿĀ'ishah is negating a hadith which encourages kindness to animals; there is a great deal of other statements regarding the Prophet's kind treatment of animals, particularly cats, that can be used to inculcate such behaviour in believers. But what she is taking exception to is that such a notion could be spread in a manner that insinuates that this could be the fate of a believing woman who has spent her life in prayer, charity, and other acts of faithfulness only to have it all come to nothing by the singular misdeed of mistreating a cat. Hence, the need to clarify the woman had many sins to her name, most seriously, that she denied Allah. Perhaps what was particularly egregious to ʿĀ'ishah ﵂ is that if an example were to be made of anyone over their singular acts of cruelty, then surely there are better candidates than a woman, who had relatively little social, economic, or political power, especially at that time. Ultimately, the fate of a believer and their position with Allah in the realm of the unseen is unknown and immeasurable by other humans, because we do not know everything as Allah does, and it is not our position or place to stand in judgement of our fellow sisters and brothers in Islam.

Whoever loves to meet Allah, Allah loves to meet them

On the authority of Abū Hurayrah ﵁ who said:

> The Messenger of Allah ﷺ said, 'Whoever loves to meet Allah, Allah loves to meet him, and whoever hates to meet Allah, then Allah hates to meet him.' Shurayḥ said, 'I went to ʿĀ'ishah and said, "O Mother of the Believers, I heard Abū Hurayrah mention that the Messenger of Allah ﷺ made a statement, which if true, then we are ruined!"' She said, 'The

> [one claiming] ruination is the one ruined, and what was this?' He said, 'The Messenger of Allah ﷺ said, "Whoever loves to meet Allah, Allah loves to meet him, and whoever hates to meet Allah, then Allah hates to meet him," and there is not a single one from among us, except that he hates death.' She said, 'The Messenger of Allah ﷺ did say this, but when the eyes become glazed, the chest begins to rattle, the skin starts to goosebump and the fingers begin to twitch, then, at this point, whoever loves to meet Allah, Allah loves to meet him, and whoever hates to meet Allah, Allah hates to meet him.'[45]

The fear of Shurayḥ, upon hearing that whoever hates to meet Allah, Allah hates to meet them, was one that was shared by ʿĀ'ishah ﷺ when she first heard the Prophet ﷺ mention this. At the time she had also asked, 'Messenger of Allah, does hating to meet Allah mean hating to meet death? For all of us hate death.' The Prophet ﷺ replied:

> No. Rather that is only at the moment of death. But if he is given the glad tidings of the mercy and forgiveness of Allah, he loves to meet Allah and Allah loves to meet him; and if he is given the tidings of the punishment of Allah, he hates to meet Allah and Allah hates to meet him.[46]

Death is naturally abhorrent to human beings, believers or not. We have spent so much of our time building lives, families, friendships, communities, and homes in this world. Even if we have simultaneously been investing in our hereafters, the difficulty of leaving what is present and familiar for that which is unseen, and unknown creates apprehension. However, the Prophet ﷺ clarifies that for the believer death is just a necessary milestone on the journey to Allah. It is like a door through which they see what awaits. Once the door is open, they can see what is on the other side, so that before they have even walked through it, they are either pleased or frightened to proceed.

This sentiment of momentary dislike of death only to be comforted quickly by the knowledge of what lies ahead was beautifully captured by the famous Bengali poet Rabindranath Tagore when he wrote, 'And because I love this life, I know I shall love death as well. The child cries out when from the right breast the mother takes it away, in the very next moment to find in the left one its consolation.'[47]

The Prophet's ascension to Allah

Al-Bukhārī and Muslim record:

> Masrūq asked ʿĀ'ishah ﵂ if the Prophet ﷺ had indeed seen Allah on the day of his ascension, the *mirāj* to the seventh heavens. ʿĀ'ishah ﵂ responded, 'You have made my

hairs stand on end by what you have uttered. Who has said to you that Muhammad ﷺ saw his Lord, for he has certainly lied.' She went on to recite from the Qur'an: *No vision can grasp Him, but His grasp is over all vision; He is above all comprehension, yet is acquainted with all things* (*al-Anʿām* 6:103), to then state: 'Rather, he saw Jibrā'īl in his natural form twice.'

In another tradition it is recorded that ʿĀ'ishah ﷺ was respectfully challenged for her view on this matter and asked what then did the Qur'an mean when it says: *and he [Muhammad] has seen him on a clear horizon and he [Muhammad] certainly saw him on another descent*'(*al-Takwīr* 81: 23) She explained, 'I am the first of this community of Muslims to question the Messenger of Allah about this and he said, "It was in fact Jibrā'īl, whom I did not see in his natural form on any occasion other than these two."'

There is a general consensus amongst classical scholars that the Prophet ﷺ did not in fact see Allah with his eyes when he ascended the heavens. ʿĀ'ishah ﷺ and others from amongst the senior Companions contended any claims to the contrary. But it is worth pondering what it would mean to see Allah. In the Qur'an, Allah proclaims: *Some faces that Day will be shining and radiant, looking upon their Lord* (*al-Qiyāmah* 75: 22–23). In his *tafsīr* of this verse, Ibn Kathīr posits that the believers' faces will be beautified by the joy and cheer that is brought to them upon resting their gaze on their Creator. I invite you to pause to imagine this. When I look upon the faces of my children, I often feel my heart swell and a tender calm settle upon me. I can feel my limbs relax and the diffusion of oxytocin through my body. This is the closest earthly experience I can refer to that could give me some measure of what awaits us: a joy activated by a vision so powerful that it has a physical effect on our bodies.

In another narration recorded by al-Bukhārī, Jarīr reports that one cloudless night, he along with some other Companions sat with the Prophet ﷺ. The full moon glowed in its resplendent glory as it hung in the sky, drawing all their gazes to it. The Prophet ﷺ then said, 'You will certainly see your Lord as you see this moon, and there will be no trouble in seeing Him. So, if you can avoid missing a prayer from the rising of the sun [Fajr] and before its setting [ʿAsr] you must do so.' The Prophet ﷺ then recited the following verse: *and glorify the Praises of your Lord, before the rising of the sun and its setting* (*Qāf* 50: 39).

Imagine that. The sight of our Lord as clear as the irresistible sight of a full moon. Let the very sight of a full moon invoke in us a reminder of the Day in which some will be favoured with a sighting of Allah, and some will not. May Allah grant us the *tawfīq* to be amongst those who are honoured with this Divine vision, *āmīn*.

4

ʿĀ'ishah's Political Influence: Her Siyasah Sharʿiyyah

The role of women in leadership positions and, in particular, political roles has been highly contested, and yet history attests to Muslim women's engagement in all spheres of public and private life, including politics. Indeed, in the Qur'an too we find great praise of Bilqīs, better known as the Queen of Sheba, in Surah Saba', as a leader who imbibed wisdom and foresight—qualities that are pertinent for successful leadership.

We know that the Prophet ﷺ consulted his wives on all matters including political ones. His home was a hub for discussion concerning management of the affairs of the growing Muslim community. ʿĀ'ishah ؓ would have grown up having heard and witnessed such conversations first in her own home as the daughter of Abu Bakr and then in her husband's home as the wife of the Prophet. Intelligent, far-sighted, wise, and influential, she continued to be of service to her father and Umar ibn al-Khaṭṭāb as each fulfilled his respective years as Caliph.

Umar saw to it that she was granted a larger allowance than the other wives of the Prophet in keeping with her privileged position with the Prophet but also in keeping with her stature and influence, and as appreciation for the guidance that she provided. During Uthman ibn ʿAffān's reign she became a vocal critic of his as accusations of nepotism emerged against him. She was also grief stricken when Uthman was brutally murdered and called for those responsible to be held to account. When she felt that Ali was failing in his duty to do so, she mobilised a campaign to hold him to account for his responsibility to bring Uthman's murderers to justice.

Ali too was in the unenviable position of taking up leadership at a time when the community was deeply fractured and divisions simmered threatening to spill into violence, whilst opportunists waited in the wings hoping for such violence to erupt in order to take advantage themselves. Ultimately, ʿĀ'ishah supported by the people of Makkah, with her cousin Ṭalḥa ibn ʿUbayd Allah and brother-in-law, al-Zubayr ibn al-ʿAwwām, as her generals, gathered an army against Ali. This episode was to come to be known as the *Fitnah*. Though she would ultimately be defeated in battle, she exemplified the possibility of Muslim women being involved in all spheres of life, to take risks, to hold their leaders to account, and to sometimes fail in their strategies just as their male counterparts do.

Her commitment to the Sunnah

> When unrest towards Uthman ibn ʿAffan's leadership grew and he sought to shut down descent, ʿĀ'ishah spoke out, holding items belonging to the beloved Messenger of Allah in her hand proclaiming, 'How soon indeed you have forgotten the practice of your Prophet, and these, his hair, shirt, and sandal have not yet perished.'[48]

With these words Uthman, the leader of the community of believers, was chastened and retracted his command to prevent the gatherings of dissent that were taking place at the home of Umm Salamah. Famed for her incisive advising of the Prophet after the Treaty of Hudaybiyyah, Umm Salamah's home had become a hub for people gathering to voice discontent regarding some of Uthman's decisions, particularly regarding who he put in positions of power.

Likewise, the Andalusian scholar Imam Aḥmad ibn Muhammad ibn ʿAbd Rabihi al-Andalusi records

ʿĀ'ishah as having said, 'May Allah have mercy on Labīd[49], he would say, "Gone are those under whose shadows life is found, and what remains are those who are followed, are like scabby skin," what would he make of this time of ours now?'[50] Just a few decades after the passing of the Prophet whilst those who were present as the Qur'an was revealed still lived, they were already lamenting the drift away from the sublime message and lofty principles with which the Prophet led his people and towards which he raised their standards. Out of sheer frustration, ʿĀ'ishah gathered the few physical remnants she had of the Prophet and holding them high chastised her people for being led astray by worldly pursuits and foregoing the way exemplified by the noble Messenger of Allah. Sadly, this seems to have become the lament of each generation.

ʿĀ'ishah's speech upon hearing of Uthman's murder

Imam al-Ṭabarī records that ʿĀ'ishah was in Makkah when Uthman was murdered in Madinah. At first, she decided to embark on her return to Madinah but then decided to return to Makkah where she stood before the Ḥajr al-Aswad on the eastern wall of the Kaaba and called out to the people who were in dismay and shock at the news. She raised her powerful voice and addressed the people eloquently, stating:

People of Makkah! The mob of men from the garrison cities and the watering places and the slaves of the people of Madinah have conspired together. They have charged this man who was killed yesterday with deceit, with putting young men in high positions where older ones had been before, and with reserving certain specially protected places for them, although they had been arranged before him and could not properly be changed. Nevertheless, he went along with these people, and in an attempt to pacify them he withdrew from these policies. When they could find neither real argument nor excuse, they became irrational. They showed their hostility openly, and their deeds did not match their words. They spilled forbidden blood, they violated the sacred city, they appropriated sacred money, and they profaned the sacred month.

By Allah! One of Uthman's fingers is better than a whole world of their type. Save yourselves from being associated with them, let others punish them and let their followers be scared off. By Allah! Even if what they reckon against him were a crime, he would have been cleared of it, as gold is cleaned of its impurities or a garment of its dirt, for they have rinsed him [in his own blood] as a garment is rinsed in water.[51]

ʿĀ'ishah ﷺ always spoke up for the truth. When she was rebuked by Abū al-Aswad for her taking Ali ﷺ to account for not bringing Uthman's murders to justice citing her own vocal objection to some of his policies, she rebuked him saying:

> We were angry at him for his beatings with the whip, his setting aside rain land enclosures, and appointing Saʿīd and al-Walīd governors. But you assaulted him and desecrated three sacred rights; the sanctity of the town [Madinah], the sanctity of the Caliphate, and the sanctity of the holy month, after we had washed him as a vessel is washed and he had become clean. Thus, you perpetrated this offence on him wrongfully. Should we get angry on your behalf at the whip of Uthman and not get angry on behalf of Uthman at your sword?[52]

ʿĀ'ishah ﷺ was not swayed by political ties nor personal gain, a perfect exemplar of Islamic leadership. If she took Uthman ﷺ to task for the criticisms voiced by the people, then she would also do the same with Ali ﷺ and his inertia in bringing Uthman's murders to account. She exudes integrity, courage, and commitment to the Sunnah of the Prophet ﷺ and the message of the Qur'an. Her commitment was always to the triumph of Islam and the principles held sacred in the life of a believer. That is what makes her a radiant example for anyone seeking entry into politics or indeed any position that requires dealing with diverse peoples, opinions, and abilities.

ʿĀ'ishah's letter of appeal to the Kufans

Al-Ṭabarī records ʿĀ'ishah's letter to the Kufans to petition them for support stating:

> After greetings, I am reminding you of Allah and Islam. Uphold the Book of Allah by carrying out its command: "Be concious of Allah, and hold on tight to His rope"[53]...We came to Basrah, and we appealed to its people to uphold the Book of Allah by carrying out Allah's punishments, but the feckless received us with weapons and said, "We will cause you to follow Uthman [ibn ʿAffan]."[54] They did this to avoid establishing the boundaries of Allah. They rebelled and accused us of unbelief and spoke badly to us. So, we recited the Qur'anic verse: "Do you not consider those who were given a portion of the Scripture? They are invited to the Scripture of Allah that it should arbitrate between them; then a party of them turns away, and they are refusing."[55] Some of them acknowledged me but disagreed amongst themselves so we let them be. But this didn't prevent the hostile amongst them from drawing their swords against my people.

'Uthman ibn Ḥunayf insisted that their only course of action was to fight me, but Allah protected me with devout men, and He threw their trickery back in their faces...O people of Kufa, do not withdraw your approval from anyone except the killers of Uthman ibn ʿAffan...do not argue on behalf of traitors and do not facilitate the weakening of Allah's limits. I warn you to protect you from joining the ranks of the unjust...We were calling them to the truth and urging them not to intervene between us and the truth, but they practiced deception and treachery. We did not do the same."[56]

This is an abridged version of a much longer letter in which ʿĀ'ishah ﷺ relays details of the *fitnah* thus far from her perspective. It is rich with historical detail and illustrates the depth of ʿĀ'ishah's religious knowledge and political prowess. There are many lessons embedded within it. Indeed, it could be argued that this letter alone could easily be the subject of an entire essay. No doubt, the perceptive reader will find many insights for themselves in addition to what is pointed out here.

Recognising that she needed support for her army when she arrived in Basrah, ʿĀ'ishah ﷺ sent out letters to the leaders of various provinces and tribes. The letter presented here was the one she sent to the people of Kufa, Iraq. She communicates clearly, with great articulation and emotive language. It would be difficult for any recipient of this letter to have denied this Mother of the Believers her petition. It is not surprising that her eloquence has gone down in history. Imam al-Tirmidhī records in his *Sunan* that Mūsā ibn Ṭalḥah said, 'I have not seen anyone more eloquent than ʿĀ'ishah', and others have said that a single speech of ʿĀ'ishah's was more beneficial than numerous Friday sermons for the valuable knowledge, insight and wisdom which they contained and the clarity, power and oratory with which she delivered.

Al-Aḥnāf ibn Qays ﵁ is recorded in the *Siyar Aʿlām al-Nubalā'* as saying, 'I heard the *khuṭbah* of Abu Bakr, Umar, Uthman, Ali and caliphs after them, but I never heard speech from the mouth of any creature more eloquent and more perfect than that from the mouth of ʿĀ'ishah.' It is for this and her leadership qualities that it was said by Abū Ḥayyān al-Tawhīdī, 'If her father, al-Ṣiddīq, had a son the likes of ʿĀ'ishah, the leadership (i.e., the Khilāfah) would not have left his family.'[57]

Etiquette of war

> On the day of the Battle of the Camel, ʿĀ'ishah ﵂ counselled her people saying, 'Disputing during battle is weakness, and crying during battle is cowardly.'[58]

Civil unrest in the first few decades—centuries even—of Islam was not uncommon. Innumerable battles were fought; many were won, and many were lost. But nothing was comparable to the fissure and chaos created by the brutal demise of Uthman ibn ʿAffān and its aftermath. This left many Muslims in a state of shock and confusion. With the respected cousin and son-in-law Ali pitted against ʿĀ'ishah, the beloved wife of the Prophet, it is little wonder that the community of Muslims felt their loyalties scattered and their steadfastness routinely shaken. When ʿĀ'ishah saw this emerge within the ranks of her army she knew that it had to be addressed because an army is only as strong as its conviction; muscle and weaponry are secondary matters when battles are fought on equal terms, as the Muslims witnessed at Badr when they were outnumbered by their enemy manyfold but still fought to victory. ʿĀ'ishah exhorted her soldiers to strength and steadfastness now that the battle lines were drawn, and they had come forth to fight for the side which they had agreed was closer to truth.

Whilst ʿĀ'ishah's advice was delivered in the context of war, there is a wisdom beyond battle for us all to benefit from which is the call to *iḥsān*; excellence in all that we commit ourselves to. The Prophet said, 'Allah, the Majestic is excellent and loves excellence.'[59] When a Muslim sets out to complete a task then, it should be done to the highest standard because that is what is beloved to Allah.

The poetry of ʿĀ'ishah ﵂ and her army

When the camel upon which ʿĀ'ishah ﵂ was seated became the target for Alī's army, ʿĀ'ishah ﵂ called out to keep the morale of her soldiers buoyed. Imam al-Ṭabarī narrates:

> [ʿĀ'ishah] asked the man on her left, 'Who are these?' 'Your sons al-Azd,' replied Sabrah ibn Shaymān. 'Tribesmen of Ghassān!' She called out, 'We used to hear of your prowess with the sword; keep it up today!' And she quoted the poetry verses, 'The Ghassāni protectors fought with their swords, as did Hinb and Aws and Shabīb.' She then asked the man on her right, 'Who are these?' 'Bakr ibn Wā'il,' he replied. She said, 'It was of you the poet said, "He came at us with swords and armour as though they were judging from their impenetrable strength, Bakr ibn Wā'il."'[60]

Perhaps even more moving is the reply of her soldiers who matched her poetry with their own crying out, 'O Mother of ours, ʿĀ'ishah, do not fear! All your sons are brave heroes. No one among us is anxious or [over]cautious.'[61]

To be proficient in poetry was a mark of refinement, education, and culture. That ʿĀ'ishah ﵂ was able to recite powerful and inspiring poetry in an impromptu manner about each of the tribes that fought valiantly around her is testimony to her intelligence, but also to her quick-wittedness and her ability to steer her people with confidence and clarity despite the perilousness of the situation. A good leader needs to inspire and bring out the best in their people, one who can identify, highlight and uplift their strengths and qualities to create an environment of positivity and confidence despite the odds. Regardless that the palanquin in which she sat upon her camel was so utterly riddled with arrows and spears that it was described as looking like a hedgehog, ᶜĀ'ishah ﵂ was still able to rise to the moment with courage and uphold all these qualities of a great leader.

ᶜĀ'ishah's warning to Muᶜāwiyah ﵁

> When Muᶜāwiyah ﵁ became Caliph, ᶜĀ'ishah ﵂ wrote to him saying, 'When a man does what is hateful to Allah, those among the people who had first praised him will then reproach him.'[62]

The circumstances which caused ᶜĀ'ishah ﵂ to send this comment to Muᶜāwiyah ﵁ remains unclear. No context is provided in the history books, but it is presented as an example of her concise wisdom. Clearly, this was one of the principles by which she lived life, and perhaps even a lesson she witnessed while living among the people. After all, she had seen four Caliphs before him and numerous ministers and representatives of theirs come and go.

There are two ways in which this statement can be interpreted. The first is the importance of the community (*jamāʿah*) and to not stray from it because the *ummah* is one that has been described in the Qur'an as being composed of each other's protectors and friends. Those who are sincere to their leader will praise them when they do well and reproach them when they do wrong. As Allah has proclaimed: *Indeed, all of humankind is in utter loss, except for those who believe and work righteous deeds, and advise one another to the truth and advise one another to patience* (*al-ʿAṣr* 103: 2–3).

A second way of reading this piece of advice is that one must always stay committed to the way of Allah, for praise and rebukes are not important; if an individual performs actions that are hateful to Allah and finds that they are praised for it, then sooner or later the same people who praised that individual will also collude to bring them down. Perhaps the most common experience of this can be found in our childhoods. How often did we find ourselves urged on by friends to steal a sweet or cheat on a test or any other such misdeeds which we urge each other towards in our childish naivety, only to find those same friends cheering us on are often the first to expose us to the adults in our lives once caught. Whilst as children this can be endearing and the source of valuable life lessons, as adults people-pleasing cannot be the mode by which we operate, especially when we hold positions of authority.

Ultimately though, for the Muslim striving to be closer to Allah, their loyalty is to the truth, no matter the number of those who oppose them. The eleventh-century Andalusian scholar Ibn Hazm wrote in his *al-Ihkām fī Usūl al-Ahkām*, 'The *jamāʿah* is in reference to the people of truth. Even if there is only one of them in the entire world, they will be referred to as the *jamāʿah*. When Abu Bakr and Khadijah became Muslims, only they and the Prophet ﷺ were the *jamāʿah*, and everyone else in the world was separated from the *jamāʿah*.' Likewise, Ibn al-Qayyim shared the words of the Damascene historian, Abū Shāmah on the matter where he stated to hold onto the *jamāʿah* 'means clinging to the truth and following it even if those who are holding onto it are few while those opposing it are many. This is because the truth is what the first *jamāʿah* was on from the time of the Prophet ﷺ and the Ṣaḥābah.'

The Muslim who finds themselves in such a position of responsibility has to find a fine balance between consulting with the people, so as not to become tyrannical and narrow-minded, while foremostly remaining loyal to Allah, such that the people's influence does not transgress the boundaries of what is just, moral and closest to *taqwā*.

5

'Ā'ishah on Heart Softeners, Al-Raqā'iq

*T*he world pushes us towards wanting designer labels, holidays in far flung destinations, and luxury cars. It entices us with the promise of clout and status as it enslaves us to the routine of snap–caption–post–repeat, ensuring that even those who are not present to witness our material gains are made aware of them. We add filters to perfect the picture, we edit out the blemishes, but what of the heart in all of this enterprise? Along the way the heart is in danger of being filtered out too.

Allah, on the other hand, calls us to a consciousness about the state of our hearts. Something that can't be snapped, captioned, and posted on social media. An endeavour so private it sits as an intimate whisper, a promise of sincere affection and devotion between the believer and Allah, the lover and the

Beloved. Allah informs us in the Qur'an, *The Day whereon neither wealth nor sons shall avail, only the one who comes to Allah with a sound heart* (*al-Shuʿarā'* 26: 88–89). All the delights of the world that transform into a source of arrogant pride, wealth, and children—particularly sons in a patriarchal society—are often the Achille's heel of far too many of us. The value of a sound heart cannot be overstated, and so it is with this Divine warning that ʿĀ'ishah's statements are now presented.

The Prophet ﷺ would choose the easiest of what is permissible

It is reported that ʿĀ'ishah ؓ said:

> The Messenger of Allah ﷺ was never presented with two choices except that he would choose the easier of the two, as long as it was not a sin, in which case he would be the furthest of all people from it. And nor did the Messenger of Allah ever take revenge on account of his own self, unless the limits of Allah had been transgressed, in which case he would take revenge for Allah.[63]

When Allah ﷻ revealed the verses of Surah al-Baqarah prescribing the fast of Ramadan upon the *ummah* of Muhammad ﷺ, He said: *Indeed Allah wishes for you ease, and does not wish for you hardship* (*al-Baqarah* 2: 185). In explaining this verse, the twelfth-century exegete Fakhr al-Dīn al-Rāzi beautifully brings to our attention that even when Allah ordained this central pillar of Islam, He prioritised ease. Allah chose only one month out of twelve, and of that month He only asked for the daylight hours, not the days and the nights, and of those days He made exceptions for those who are travelling or sick.

In Arabic the words used by Allah for ease and hardship are اليسر and العسر, respectively. For those with knowledge of Arabic, you will recognise that both words are preceded by the definite article, ال. This would translate as 'the ease' and 'the hardship'. This would make for a grammatically incorrect translation in English, but al-Rāzi points out that the definite article stands for the boundaries of this ease and hardship as falling within the parameters of what Allah has made permissible and beneficial for Muslims. And, as always, we see this best exemplified in the behaviour of the Prophet ﷺ who sought out ease, cognizant of the fact that his *ummah* would strive to emulate his perfect example, but always remaining within the sanctuary of Allah's parameters.

And yes, it is a sanctuary that is to be found within Allah's parameters. In another verse of the Qur'an, Allah ﷻ declares:

> *Those who follow the Messenger, the unlettered Prophet, he whom they find written with them in the Torah and the Gospel, commands*

them to all that is known to be good and prohibits them from all that is bad and makes lawful for them all that is pure and makes unlawful for them all that is foul, and removes from them their burdens and the shackles that were upon them. So those who believe in him, support him, vindicate him and follow the Light that has been revealed upon him, they are the successful ones (*al-Aʿrāf* 7: 157).

Beloveds, let's ponder this verse. Those who follow the way of Muhammad ﷺ are guided to all that is good and that which exceeds the standards of society in any time and place, elevating each person and delivering them to full dignity. Those who follow him are protected from the evils of the world that reduce a human being to the lowest of all creatures, demeaned and wretched. But then Allah says, most pertinently, that shackles and burdens are removed. What are these shackles and burdens? Surely amongst them is to be enslaved to our desires, to the false systems of oppression constructed by men of greed and insatiable desires, the burdens that are ours when we feel stripped of our agency and humanity.

What joy is found in following the example of a prophet who stayed focused on the Oneness and Supremacy of Allah alone, and with that found strength to overcome the oppressors of his time, whilst being patient with that which was outside of his control and lay within the remit of Allah only, and to do so all while being mindful of the boundaries Allah has set for Muslims. It is within Allah's parameters that we seek to remain and not those of society, rulers and leaderships, who would situate themselves as partners with Allah. We seek refuge in Allah from committing the unforgivable sin of shirk, *āmīn*.

The Prophet ﷺ loved to show gratitude to Allah

> ʿĀ'ishah ◌ recounted that the Prophet ﷺ would stand for long durations of time in prayer such that the skin on his feet would crack. One day, she said, 'I asked him, "Why do you do this, Messenger of Allah, when you have been forgiven the former and latter of your sins?" To which he replied, "Shall I not be a grateful slave of Allah?"'[64]

By way of this question the *ummah* of Muhammad ﷺ has been blessed with benefiting from his answer. It is not an angry God in need of placating whom we worship. It is not a begrudging punitive Lord to whom we forcibly submit. Unlike many of us who may be fuelled by guilt to worship Allah, the Prophet's knowledge of Allah and relationship with Him, made him acutely aware of something greater: of the Mercy, Love and Infinite Generosity of Allah. Of course, there is a great reward for seeking Allah's forgiveness and it is a deed beloved to Him, but the rewards and benefits of gratitude are profound.

Interestingly, in this hadith, the Prophet ﷺ responds, 'Shall I not be a grateful servant of Allah?' the word for grateful that he uses in Arabic is *shākir*. Allah uses both *ḥamd* and *shukr* in the Qur'an when referring to gratitude. We begin every prayer with Surah al-Fatihah, the opening words of which are *al-ḥamdu lillāh*, All Praise is for Allah, and we use these very words to thank Allah after we eat or drink, when someone asks how we are doing, when we are reminded of the blessings upon us, and yes, even in times of difficulty we thank Allah invoking these words as a reminder that even through tests we are blessed in a myriad of ways.

Allah ﷻ says in the Qur'an: *If you are grateful (shakartum), I will surely bestow on you more* (*Ibrāhīm* 14: 7). In this verse the word for showing gratitude that Allah uses is also from the same root word *shukr*. By being a grateful servant of Allah, the Prophet ﷺ was activating the promise of this verse; and how truthful is our Lord, for what is the example of the Prophet but a man that was given in abundance by Allah? A modest man of honourable but humble beginnings, without a father at his birth, fully orphaned in infancy, a man of few words given more to contemplation than conversation, who lived an ordinary almost obscure life, then chosen by Allah as a Prophet and Messenger, ostracised, boycotted, and driven out of his home. But, by the strength of his faith, the durability of his steadfastness and the resoluteness with which he remains grateful, Allah elevated him. His name evokes love and admiration centuries after his death. His name has travelled across the globe and his message has been adopted by people in the most remote lands. So many hundreds of thousands of baby boys have been named after him such that, by many accounts, Muhammad has become the most popular name in the world today. Despite the machinations of those who plotted against him in his life and thereafter, none has been able to succeed in extinguishing the light of his message or place a blemish on his name, and nor will they ever succeed. Indeed, to give thanks is to receive more of Allah's bounties, for Allah does not tire of giving.

Some Arabic linguists have said that while *ḥamd* is a verbal manifestation of gratitude, *shukr* is the expression of gratitude on the tongue and also from the heart and by one's actions. In other words, *shukr* is the highest form of gratitude that a believer can embody to express thankfulness to Allah; it is a form that has travelled deep beyond their tongues, settled in their hearts and bloomed on their limbs. To gaze upon such a person is to observe a person comfortable in their contentment, blessed with a heart that does not burn with envy and a tongue that does not strike from spite. May we all be granted hearts filled with contentment rooted in gratitude to Allah, *āmīn*.

Mercy begins at home

> It is reported by Anas ibn Mālik 🙵, that a
> poor woman had visited ʿĀʾishah 🙵 so she
> gave her three dates. The poor woman gave
> each of her two children a date to eat and
> kept the third for herself. Upon finishing their
> dates, the two children looked longingly at
> their mother. She unhesitatingly, took her
> date, split it in half and gave a piece to each
> of them. ʿĀʾishah 🙵 was so moved by what
> she witnessed, she relayed the incident to the
> Prophet 🙵 who said to her, 'Are you surprised
> at that? Allah will show her mercy because of
> her mercy towards her children.'[65]

Muslims are well acquainted with the high esteem
in which Islam holds the virtue of mercy, but family
members are rarely the first recipients of such
gentleness. Often our kindest faces are for people
outside the home whilst our most miserable faces
are sadly reserved for those within the home. How
often have we heard a Prophetic statement like the
one whereby he said, 'Allah will not be merciful to
those who are not merciful to people,' and rushed
to apply it through our exchanges with friends,
neighbours, colleagues, strangers on the streets, but
failed to establish this mercy in our own homes? One
of the words for home in Arabic is *maskan*, which
comes from the same root words as *sakīnah* (peace).

The home should be a haven of peace for its residents. But the root word means more than simply peace and tranquillity, it also indicates the ceasing of pain, anger, hurt and the like.

The world is a wonderful place, but it is also a place that can wear each one of us down in a multitude of ways; those who work, study, or simply go about their errands can often be subject to unexpected or unwarranted blows, to be left feeling ambushed and beleaguered. The home should be a place for recuperation, where we can come and rest our tired bones, and find ourselves replenished. The Prophet ﷺ was gentle in his household. His children, wives and servants did not scurry away when he entered the home. When he entered his home, the atmosphere did not darken, nor did it become severe. Instead, kindness, compassion, and charity all began and flourished in his household, and from there were able to radiate out towards the community. The home was the centre of his strength. When he first encountered Jibrā'īl ﷺ and came home shivering, delirious and fearful of having been gripped by insanity, it was his wife Khadijah ﷺ who was there to embrace him. She was the one who grabbed a blanket and wrapped it around him, holding him in her arms, bringing him close and whispering into his ears words of reassurance, 'By Allah! Allah would never disgrace you. You maintain family ties, you support the weak, you help the poor and needy, you show generosity to your guests, and you are patient in the path of truthfulness.'[66] When Khadijah ﷺ was consoling the Prophet ﷺ, the first of his virtues that she referenced was his demeanour towards family. How each of us behaves towards our family is the true measure of what each of our characters is made of.

The Prophet ﷺ was known for being magnanimous with his wives. ʿĀ'ishah ﷺ narrates of an evening when the Prophet ﷺ returned home after a day of tending to the community and its many needs. As many of us are when we return from a day at work, he was tired and hungry and was presented with a loaf of bread for dinner. ʿĀ'ishah ﷺ recalls the feeling of inadequacy that came over her when the Prophet ﷺ asked for something to accompany the bread, and all they had available was some vinegar. Vinegar, the sourest of all condiments. Feeling some shame as she presented it to her husband, and disappointed that she could not have responded with something more substantial, she was heartened when this beautiful man dipped the bread into the vinegar cheerfully and exclaimed, 'What an excellent condiment vinegar is!'[67] This is mercy: to feel one's own disappointment but to see the efforts of one's loved ones and to make sure those were prioritised, to know one's own power but to choose kindness, to serve the comfort of your family over your own.

The rights of a neighbour

> ʿĀ'ishah reported that the Prophet confided in her that, 'Jibrā'īl continually recommended that I treat neighbours well until I thought that they would be designated inheritance.'[68]

In another hadith narrated by ʿĀ'ishah she reports asking the Prophet which of her two neighbours she should send gifts to as she had enough to send a gift to only one of them. The Prophet instructed her to send it to the one closest to her. This Prophetic ethos links to the previous discussion on the importance of establishing mercy in the home, in that those in closest proximity to us are most deserving of our best self. Just like the roots of a tree need to be firm and strong for it to be able to reach its highest potential, so too the individual must be committed to their purpose of establishing Allah's sovereignty on earth. Establishing Allah's sovereignty on earth means to embody the Prophetic mission of being a force for all that is good and just in this world.

There is also a radical notion to be found in the combination of this hadith and the one in the previous section. How often have we looked upon a figure from history or in the world today who has sacrificed so much for the betterment of others, only to find that their own families rank amongst their sacrifices? How many an individual have set forth from their homes with the intention and commitment to great objectives, only to neglect the people closest to them? How many a scholar, teacher, activist, or humanitarian have spent their lives serving communities around the world, all the while remaining strangers to their own families and neighbours?

In the Prophet ﷺ we find the opposite; a man who did not seek the limelight, who did not seek stages and auditoriums, who did not seek audiences and renown. A man who was content in the quiet *khalwah*, isolation with God in the mountain of Hira, who—had he not been selected as the Prophet and Messenger of God—would have happily continued in his simple life of devotion and honesty. A man who, when he was called to fulfil the Prophetic mission, did not then neglect his family nor his neighbours. He did not exclude them in order to expand the body of the believers. He did not place his family or neighbours second but first, always first. We now see the result of the Prophet's way: a family who loved him and continued to forge forward with his mission, neighbours who became Muslims after much animosity and aggression towards him, all because he remained kind and caring towards them. We can look around now and see millions of believers still devoted to his message. To follow the way of the Prophet ﷺ is to know that all goodness begins in the home and with those closest to us, and that the desire to spread one's name even towards the most noble of causes runs the risk of becoming an ego trap and comes at the cost of one's own family and nearest and dearest.

The perfect character of the Prophet ﷺ

> Yazīd ibn Babnus reported that a group had approached ʿĀ'ishah and asked her what the character of the Prophet ﷺ was. She replied, 'His character was the Qur'an. Can you recite the chapter, al-Mu'minūn (The Believers)? Recite, *It is the believers who are successful: those who are humble in their prayer, those who turn away from worthless talk, those who pay the zakāh, and who guard their chastity* (*al-Mu'minūn* 23: 1–5). That was the character of the Messenger of Allah ﷺ.'[69]

When asked how the character of the Prophet ﷺ was, ʿĀ'ishah has told us quite simply, his character was that of the Qur'an in glorious embodiment. She explained in her selection of the first few verses of Surah al-Mu'minūn some of the actions in which he was engaged: showing humility in prayer, refraining from idle conversations, paying the required charity, and guarding his chastity. But we know that the Prophet ﷺ did much more, these are but a glimpse into the praxis of the Prophet ﷺ. We know that he gave more than the required *zakāh* payments in charity, we know he spent long nights in prayer, that he fought *jihād* in the path of Allah, that he comforted the weak, provided refuge to orphans, arbitrated justly in the affairs of his people. We know that the Qur'an makes many demands on the attentive believer, so how can we too strive to do so?

Allah ﷻ says in the Qur'an,

وَإِذَا قُرِئَ ٱلْقُرْءَانُ فَٱسْتَمِعُوا۟ لَهُۥ وَأَنصِتُوا۟ لَعَلَّكُمْ تُرْحَمُونَ ﴿٢٠٤﴾

(الاعراف ٧: ٢٠٤)

When the Qur'an is recited then listen to it (istamiʿū) and be quiet (anṣitū)so that you may experience mercy (*al-Aʿrāf* 7: 204).

Allah directs us how to relate to the Qur'an so that we too may be able to embody it. When it is being recited or when we are reading it, then we should seek to truly listen to it. Some things are lost in translation, but we can interpret this short verse as deeply instructive if we exert a little effort. The first word Allah uses is *istamiʿū*. The more common way to instruct a group of people to listen would be to say, *ismaʿū*, listen! But, rather poetically, Allah has used a conjugation of the root word that indicates not only listen to the Qur'an but to *strive* to listen; to really hear each word as it is announced. The second word Allah uses is *anṣitū,* most often translated as 'an order to be quiet', but this single word holds so much more meaning. It also means to listen, but it implies listening as if you were eavesdropping.

Imagine how one behaves when trying to listen in on a conversation nearby: we make ourselves still in every way, slow down or even pause our every movement, we silence the other sounds around us. Likewise, we are reminded in this verse to pay attention and exert our efforts towards listening to Allah's magnificent Words, to silence any other interventions or interruptions between us and Allah, for this is a faith that has done away with the middlemen who would seek to impose themselves as conduits between us and Allah, such that we hear not only the literal utterances but also the secrets hidden in the layers of their eternal meanings.

The next time you read or hear the Qur'an, dear reader, still your mind and body, shut out the other sounds around you, lock out all intrusive thoughts and let the Words of Allah truly speak to you so that not only have your ears received them but the Words have poured into your heart causing it to expand at the glory of Allah. Only then does the believer experience the contentment, joy, and ecstasy of the promise of Mercy that Allah ends this verse with.

On controlling the tongue

> ʿĀ'ishah ﵂ relays an incident whereby a group of Jews would come to the Prophet ﷺ and not iterate their greetings of *salām* clearly instead saying *'al-sāmu 'alaykum'* meaning may poison be upon you. ʿĀ'ishah ﵂ says,

'I understood what they had said, so I responded, "May poison be upon you, and the curse of Allah!" The Messenger of Allah ﷺ said, "Slow down, ʿĀ'ishah! Allah loves gentleness in all our affairs." I said, "But Messenger of Allah didn't you hear what they were saying?" The Messenger of Allah ﷺ said, "I already said to them, and upon you (*wa 'alaykum*)."'[70]

In the beginning of Surah al-Rahmān, we read that The Merciful taught the Qur'an, created humankind, revealed to them how to communicate, set the sun and the moon in their appointed courses, whilst the stars in the sky and trees on the earth all bowed in awe of Him, and then Allah finally says that He raised the sky high and devised for all things a balance (*mīzān*). The Prophet ﷺ in this example, which is also cited by ʿĀ'ishah ﵂, guided by his awareness of Allah's All-Encompassing knowledge and perfect justice, wary not to upset the balance of the scales of justice against himself, demonstrates a life lived in harmony. This was something the Prophet ﷺ encouraged his followers to be steadfast upon too. In a similar situation but this time with ʿĀ'ishah's father, Abu Bakr al-Ṣiddīq ﵁, one that is recorded in the Musnad of Imam Aḥmad, tells that Abu Bakr was seated with the Prophet ﷺ, when a man approached him and started to verbally abuse Abu Bakr. Abu Bakr ﵁ ignored the man's profanities, and the Prophet ﷺ sat smiling. But the man transgressed the limits of Abu Bakr's patience until he responded as any of us would have, by rebuking the man and returning his hurtful words to him. At this point, the Prophet ﷺ, looking disdainful, got up to leave. Abu Bakr ؓ was astonished and said to him, 'Messenger of Allah, this man reviled me, and you were sitting, but when I responded you got angry and got up to leave.' The Prophet ﷺ said, 'There was an angel with you responding on your behalf, but when you responded with the same words as he, a devil appeared, and I will not sit in the presence of a devil.'

For the believer there are always two concerns: one is that they trust Allah to deliver perfect justice and restore the cosmic balance in their affairs; but the second is that they have a consciousness of Allah's watchfulness, aware that just as they rely on Allah to repair injustices against them, there are others against whom they may transgress, thus causing the restoration of justice to be demanded from them. The limb that is most harmful to us in this endeavour is the tongue. The Prophet ﷺ warned that 'the greatest propensity for good or for evil in a person lies between their two lips [i.e., their tongue].'[71]

It is better to stay silent and endure with patience, than to speak words of unbridled anger. It is better to walk away from the foolish and it is better to trust in Allah to restore the balance than to unjustly wield the tongue like a sword thrashing without skill, accuracy, or planning. There is a time and a way to speak up. The Prophet ﷺ was the foremost in speaking out against ills, but he was the first to remove himself from gossip, slander, and abusive and idle talk. For that he relied on Allah and likewise encouraged his followers.

The aftereffects of words travel far beyond the moment in which they are uttered. For this reason, the great Muslim jurist and poet Mawlana Jalāl al-Dīn Rūmī stated, 'Regard the words you utter with your tongue, A dangerous arrow which you have just flung; An arrow can't be brought back from its course—we have to block the torrent at its source.'[72] If we can identify that our words can cause terrible harm to others, it is wise to meditate over them before casting them out. Allah ﷻ strikes for us a most perfect metaphor when He says: *Have you not considered how Allah sets forth an example of a good word as a good tree; its roots are firm, its branches reaching to the sky? It gives fruits in every season by the permission of its Rabb.* Most trees will bear fruit during one or two seasons of the year, but a good word bears fruit all year round. There is no time in which a good word, a word of kindness, enlightenment, encouragement, mercy, justice is not fruitful. The verse continues with Allah stating: *The example of a bad word is like that of a bad tree. Its roots are uprooted upon the earth, it has no stability* (*Ibrāhīm* 14: 24–27).

How common it is for people consumed by the ego and emboldened by the individualist self-serving society that we live in to 'throw shade', to cast out words of harm and aspersions, tearing down but building nothing, leaving themselves and those around them uprooted and unstable, forever unmoored; neither feeling supported nor capable of supporting others.

On gentleness

> ʿĀʾishah ◈ mentioned, 'I was riding a camel which was being difficult and the Prophet ◈ remarked, "You must be compassionate for nothing is done with compassion except that it is beautified, and nothing is bereft of gentleness except that it is disgraced."'[73]

Gentleness was the mode of operation by which the noble Messenger Muhammad ◈ lived his life: leaving a cat to sleep on his prayer mat so as not to disturb it; rebuking Companions who had caused distress to a mother bird by having removed her chicks from their nest; was a comforting, helpful and cheerful presence in his home; who visited the ill, comforted the destitute; and provided shelter for the homeless.

The Prophet ◈ embodied gentleness and kindness. Both traits are less often associated with wit, strength and intelligence, and are more often conflated with weakness and foolishness such that many of us can often find ourselves eschewing kindness and gentleness lest we be labelled fools, lest people think we can be taken advantage of, lest people think we are imbeciles incapable of control and order. But it takes intelligence and patience of immense depth to show kindness and gentleness. It takes a great deal of skill and emotional intelligence. It requires the ability to detach from yourself and the moment to ask, is there a better way? It is the ability to see the broader picture; the interconnections of people and the world around us.

In the example given by ʿĀʾishah ⬥, soothing an unsettled animal, giving it a break for rest, stopping to see if it is being agitated by something, investigating if it might need food or water or perhaps its load is too heavy for it, questioning if there may be a discomfort in its feet, rather than beating it and shouting at it, getting frustrated at its insubordination would benefit no one—neither ʿĀʾishah ⬥ nor the camel—nor does it illustrate much depth of thought or consideration on ʿĀʾishah's part. Gentleness allows for space to be held for consideration, for emotional connection, and for the possibility of generosity in our perspective and interpretation of events; it also gives a chance for obtaining some clarity by incrementing the time we have to process things in order to learn more about a situation.

Possibly the greatest example of this is found in our weekly Friday readings of Surah al-Kahf when

Allah reminds us of the story of Mūsā and Khiḍr. Throughout his time with Khiḍr, Mūsā was agitated and impulsive in his judgement of Khiḍr's actions. He only saw the external behaviour but did not hold himself back long enough to see the deeper wisdom. On his third strike of impetuous questioning, Khiḍr enlightened Mūsā of the wisdoms behind each of his actions. When Mūsā first sought permission to accompany Khiḍr for a number of days, Khiḍr was certain Mūsā would not have the patience to endure what he would witness during their time together. He promised repeatedly that he would not question Khiḍr, who reluctantly accepted his unlikely apprentice and they began their sojourn together.

They embarked upon a boat, kindly hosted by its owners, but upon alighting, Khiḍr heavily damaged the boat. Mūsā was aghast and swiftly expressed his indignation. Khiḍr sighed, and reminded Mūsā that he had warned him that he would be incapable of journeying with him without questioning Khidr. Mūsā gathered himself, apologised and promised to do better. Not long passed before they came across a boy and Khiḍr struck him dead! Naturally, Mūsā was shocked and exclaimed the evil criminality of what Khiḍr had done. Again, Khiḍr reminded Mūsā that in taking up his company, Mūsā had gone beyond his abilities. Mūsā apologised once more and promised Khiḍr he will find him to be more dutiful of his promise to not seek answers until Khiḍr is ready to reveal his truths to him.

Promises and resolves reinforced, they continued until they arrived at a town, weary from their travels. They sought out the hospitality of the people but instead found them to be miserly and unwelcoming, offering them nothing of food nor shelter. Cast aside, they spotted a crumbling wall on the verge of collapsing. Khiḍr approached the wall and rebuilt it. Mūsā stood flabbergasted that this man who ruined the boat belonging to people who had showed them kindness and generosity was now performing free labour for the inhospitable townsfolk. While he managed to not accuse Khiḍr of evil or criminality, he could not help but suggest, 'If you had wished, surely you could have taken wages for it.'

This was to be the final straw, the point beyond which Khiḍr would no longer allow Mūsā to travel with him, but he would show him the grace of explaining all that he had witnessed and been unable to remain patient over. He explained that the boat was the property of poor seamen and that behind them, unbeknown to them all, was the ship of a tyrannical king who usurped the boats and ships of others by force. By damaging the boat, he knew that the king would leave their boat alone, and they would be able to repair Khiḍr's damage with relative ease, and therefore keep it and continue to use the boat so important to their livelihood. As for the boy he had killed, Khiḍr had been given knowledge from

Allah that he would grow up to be an oppressive and rebellious disbeliever bringing tyranny and despair into the lives of his righteous parents, thus protecting them and others from his evil. Finally, as for his repairing the crumbling wall, he had known that it was part of the property of two orphans in the town whose honourable parents had passed away leaving the children's inheritance buried under the wall. It was feared that if the townspeople were to find it, unkind and selfish as they were, they would have stolen the inheritance. As such, it was Allah's Will that the treasure remained covered until they reached adulthood and the strength to claim and keep their rightful inheritance without threat of theft.

This story holds many wisdoms, those we know well and those we have yet to discover, hence the encouragement to read it weekly. Among the lessons of patience, trusting Allah's wisdom, knowing that there is good in all our affairs ordered by Allah, perhaps we also learn the importance of gentleness and that patience is only as available to us as we are available to gentleness.

Humility

ʿĀ'ishah ﵂ said, 'When the Prophet ﷺ stood up in the night, he would start his prayer by saying:

> "Allah, Lord of Jibra'īl, Mika'īl, and Israfīl; Originator of the heavens and the earth, [and]

Knower of the hidden and the seen; You judge between Your servants concerning that which they used to differ upon, guide me through that which there has been difference upon concerning the truth by Your permission, indeed You guide whomever you wish to the Straight Path.'"[74]

اللَّهُـمَّ رَبَّ جِبْرِيـلَ وَمِيكَائِيـلَ وَإِسْرَافِيـلَ فَاطِرَ السَّمَوَاتِ وَالأَرْضِ وَعَالِمَ الْغَيْبِ وَالشَّهَادَةِ أَنْتَ تَحْكُـمُ بَيْنَ عِبَـادِكَ فِيمَا كَانُوا فِيـهِ يَخْتَلِفُونَ اهْدِنِي لِـمَا اخْتُلِفَ فِيهِ مِنَ الْحَقِّ بِإِذْنِكَ إِنَّكَ تَهْدِي مَنْ تَشَـاءُ إِلَى صِرَاطٍ مُسْتَقِيمٍ[75]

That this is the supplication of the Messenger of Allah ﷺ, is astounding. That he who had daily, direct and unmatched communication with Allah would make this *duʿāʾ* stands as a profound testimony to the humility of this noble Prophet and stands in alarming contrast to what we witness within the Muslim community far too often when religious disagreements arise.

The Prophet ﷺ is told innumerable times by Allah ﷻ in the Qur'an, both explicitly and implicitly, of his position and rank in both this world and the hereafter. His very position as the final Messenger of God is itself testimony to his uprightness in the Sight of God. If there were ever to be a person who could walk haughtily and with confidence upon the earth, surely it is Muhammad ibn ʿAbdullāh ﷺ. But no, herein lies the distinction between those who are on Allah's Path, and those who tread the path of their egos and ideologies. Those who are the servants of the Merciful walk with humility upon the earth[76]; they are those who know that transcendent and superior to all those with knowledge is the One who is All-Knowing, that while we may exert ourselves to the best of our abilities, those who have consciousness of Allah, the truly *muttaqūn* (God-conscious ones), are ever fearful of the limits of their cognitive abilities and remain watchful over their own inevitable errors, for perfection in all matters is only Allah's to claim.

All too often debate descends into chaos. Heated words transform into brandished accusations. Lines of enmity are drawn, tongues are set loose like swords unsheathed, allegations of apostasy are hurled and instead of Muslims rising into the nobility that Islam offers, they degenerate into an ugly mob. With an *ummah* of billions of people that have developed over a number of centuries, of course there will be differences, of course we will be varied and come to different conclusions at times, perhaps even contradictory ones. This is to be expected, but must it be a cause for descent, chaos, enmity? Could we not be a people with conviction and confidence in our beliefs, who can also reserve a margin for the possibility of error and change because we are chastened by a sense of humility before Allah, just as the Prophet ﷺ was?

Allah ﷻ informs us in the Qur'an: *Indeed in qiṣāṣ, there is life for you, O people of insight* (*al-Baqarah* 2: 179). *Qiṣāṣ* is often translated as laws of retribution but as Muhammad Asad points out in his translation, 'the objective of *qiṣāṣ* is the protection of the society, and not "revenge".' *Qiṣāṣ* is about the protection of *every* member of the Muslim community, which includes their mental, physical and spiritual safety. The practice and implementation of Islam should result in a life-giving force, evident by seeing every single member of the Muslim community thrive. Like a garden in bloom, where each flower and plant of varying sizes, colours, and shapes flourishes as it is quenched by water and grows tall in its reach for the sun, so too the Muslim *ummah*, with its varying peoples, languages, cultures, and histories, all flourish in their own ways, watered by the life-giving force of Islam, growing in their united effort to turn and reach towards Allah.

Abu Bakr ؓ on his deathbed

> When Abu Bakr al-Ṣiddīq ؓ was on his deathbed, ʿĀ'ishah ؓ narrates: 'He asked me, "In how many layers was the Prophet ﷺ shrouded?" I said, In three robes. He said, "Wash these two robes of mine—they were worn out—and buy me one other robe." I said, 'O father, we are wealthy.' He replied, "O daughter, the living have more right to

> the new than the dying. Only these two are suitable for the liquid pitch and pus."'[77]

Having considered the importance of humility in the life of a Muslim, this final exchange between father and daughter stands as an exemplary reminder of how humility manifested in the life of arguably the best of Muslims: Abu Bakr, who was the 'second of the two'[78] in the cave with the Prophet as they fled Makkah to make their way to Madinah, who was guaranteed paradise by the Prophet himself,[79] who was honoured with the position of the first Caliph of Islam, who fought with all his might despite his gentle character to keep the first community of believers strong and united.

Abu Bakr, who was the first to initiate the writing of the Qur'an and thereby the project of its preservation for generations to come—even he, at the time of death, despite his lifetime of achievements and guarantees, did not allow an atom's weight of arrogance to enter his heart. He does not wish to take anymore from this worldly life, eschewing new garments for burial to reuse two and accepting one more to match the Prophet in being shrouded in three garments.

When ʿĀ'ishah says that they have wealth and can afford to buy him new ones, he replies that the two old and used garments are most suitable for the 'liquid pitch and pus' alluding to the *muhl* and *ṣadīd* mentioned in the Qur'an as torments of Hell.[80]

Abu Bakr does not take for granted any of his good deeds, not even his being recognised in the Qur'an nor the many statements of the Prophet in his favour. This wasn't because he did not have full belief in these things—after all he was named al-Ṣiddīq when the Quraysh approached him to ridicule the Prophet's claim of journeying to Jerusalem, up to the seven heavens and back to Makkah in one night and he had steadfastly believed in whatever his friend said, rendering their taunts ineffective. Rather, it was his doubt and lack of confidence in his own deeds and character, fear of his own ego's machinations and above all his servitude before Allah that meant that to the very end Abu Bakr remained a humble worshipper of Allah.

The ideal *duʿā'*

> ʿĀ'ishah said that the Prophet 'used to love concise *duʿā'* and he would leave all (supplications) besides those.'[81]

In another instance, ʿĀ'ishah relayed to her half-sister Umm Kulthūm that the Prophet had come to her one day in need of something. ʿĀ'ishah was occupied with making *duʿā'* and took a long time in completing her supplications to Allah. As she continued with her *duʿā'* the Prophet said to her, "ʿĀ'ishah, make your supplications comprehensive and concise.' She said, 'When I finished, I asked,

Messenger of Allah, what is a comprehensive *duʿā*'?' He said,

> 'O Allah, I ask of you for all good, both in the present and in the future, what I know of it and what I do not. And I seek refuge in you from all evil, in the present and in the future, what I know of it and what I do not. I ask You for the Garden of Paradise and whatever speech and action draws me close to it. And I seek refuge in you from the Fire and whatever speech and action could draw me close to it. I ask you for that which Muhammad asked of you and I seek refuge in You for what Muhammad sought refuge in you from. Whatever you have preordained for me, make its end rightly guided.'

اللَّهُمَّ إِنِّي أَسْأَلُكَ مِنَ الْخَيْرِ كُلِّهِ عَاجِلِهِ وَآجِلِهِ مَا
عَلِمْتُ مِنْهُ وَمَا لَمْ أَعْلَمْ وَأَعُوذُ بِكَ مِنَ الشَّرِّ كُلِّهِ
عَاجِلِهِ وَآجِلِهِ مَا عَلِمْتُ مِنْهُ وَمَا لَمْ أَعْلَمُ وَأَسْأَلُكَ
الْجَنَّةَ وَمَا قَرَّبَ إِلَيْهَا مِنْ قَوْلٍ أَوْ عَمَلٍ وَأَعُوذُ
بِكَ مِنَ النَّارِ وَمَا قَرَّبَ إِلَيْهَا مِنْ قَوْلٍ أَوْ عَمَلٍ
وَأَسْأَلُكَ مِمَّا سَأَلَكَ بِهِ مُحَمَّدٌ صَلَّى اللهُ عَلَيْهِ وَسَلَّمَ
وَأَعُوذُ بِكَ مِمَّا تَعَوَّذَ مِنْهُ مُحَمَّدٌ صَلَّى اللهُ عَلَيْهِ وَسَلَّمَ
وَمَا قَضَيْتَ لِي مِنْ قَضَاءٍ فَاجْعَلْ عَاقِبَتَهُ رُشْدًا[81]

The way of Allah and the Messenger ﷺ is ease. He does not require—and much less desire—to thrust Muslims into difficulty. Hardship is not the marker of faith, nor burden the requirement of God. Allah tells us in the Qur'an: *Allah wills for you ease and does not will for you hardship* (al-Baqarah 2: 185). Although this was in reference to the fast of Ramadan, the precept extends to all our affairs. Likewise, we find another reminder of the importance of making ease in the Prophet's parting instruction to Muʿādh ibn Jabal رضي الله عنه as he left for Yemen to teach the people about Islam. The Prophet ﷺ said to Muʿādh رضي الله عنه, 'Make things easy and do not make things difficult. Give glad tidings and do not repel people. Cooperate with each other and do not become divided.' It is as if he said those words to us, right here, right now. In all our affairs both Allah and His Messenger ﷺ have made ease for us, most especially with regards to those actions that pertain to the *dīn*; in our making of *duʿā'*, in our fasting, praying, reciting of the Qur'an, Allah makes ease, and the noble Messenger ﷺ embodies and exemplifies it in his own practice. This is not to say that all acts of worship are easy on the first go, or that taking the path of *taqwā* is unchallenging. We all know the pain of a grumbling empty stomach in Ramadan, or the struggle to wake up at Fajr, or the struggle of wrestling the *nafs* to show compassion when one really wants to succumb to anger. But Allah is the One who grants ease, and He has promised that if you take one step towards Him, He will take ten towards you, and if you draw close to Him by a handspan, He will draw close to you by an arm's length.[83] There are two sources of ease: one is through our kindness, support and compassion for one another; and the second is the ease which Allah causes to descend as a result of those acts we do out of sincerity to Him.

The reward for reciting the Qur'an

> ʿĀ'ishah ﷺ reported that the Messenger of Allah ﷺ said, 'The one who is proficient in reciting the Qur'an will be amongst the honourable and obedient angels, and one who recites the Qur'an with difficulty but strives to recite in the best way possible, will have a double reward.'[84]

If we consider the logic of this ḥadith, the reward system is almost counter intuitive. In everyday life, whether that be work, education, or regarding any skill or talent, the master of that field is the one who is most applauded and most rewarded, the novice is barely noticed. In a class full of beginners, it is seldom anyone other than the most astute and committed learners who gain the favour and attention of the teacher. In a workplace, rarely does anyone other than the most efficient or the most productive colleague find themselves recognised. But this is not so with Allah. With Allah it is the stumbling and struggling beginner who has a double reward: a reward for committing to the task and a reward for perseverance through difficulty. More than this though, is that Allah is outside of the construct of time. While we see a beginner, Allah sees the proficient reciter, and this is a powerful thought to hold on to when we struggle with learning to read, recite, and understand the Qur'an.

When you are pushed to your limits and are tempted to give up, push yourself to visualise who you could be if you persevered a little longer and gave yourself the possibility to achieve your potential: to be who you might already be in the knowledge of Allah. Imagine yourself reciting smoothly and fluently, in a melody that is pleasing, perhaps even with understanding. Then remind yourself of the steps you need to take to get there. Watch yourself get back up after every fall, dust yourself off and start again. Triumph over the hasty self that wants fruits without the labour of sowing seeds and tending to them and set yourself to the task of labouring in the name of learning to read the Qur'an.

The blessed character of the Prophet ﷺ

> Abū ʿAbdullah al-Jadali said he asked Umm al-Mu'minīn, ʿĀ'ishah ﷺ about the character of the Prophet ﷺ. She replied saying, 'He was not obscene, nor did he revile others or

bellow in the markets. He would not return an evil with an evil but would pardon and forgive instead.'[85]

The Prophet ﷺ embodied the teachings of the Qur'an. He paved the way for Muslims and showed us through his character how best to strive. In Surah Fuṣṣilat, Allah ﷻ reminds us: *Good and evil are not equal. Repel evil by that which is better, such that the one who shows you enmity, will become like a devoted friend.* However, this is no easy task as Allah also reminds us: *But no one is able [to do this] except those who are patient, and none are able [to do this] except those who have been granted a great fortune* (*Fuṣṣilat* 41: 34–35).

Between these verses of Allah and the noble example of the Prophet ﷺ, a believer is given all they require to navigate the machinations and onslaught of those who harbour ill intentions. Even though it is difficult to respond with good to the evil of another, there are many benefits to doing so. Firstly, it protects us from acting on the worst of our interpretations of a person. As we have seen in the story of Khiḍr and Mūsā ﷺ, and perhaps as we have experienced in life, it may be that a situation appears inexcusably awful, but we may be missing key information. There may be information that explains the situation, that sheds the light required to dispel the shadows that have been cast over our hearts. It may be that our perspective and interpretation of an event, comment, or situation has been prejudiced by other experiences or information that we are incorrectly applying to this situation. By responding to an evil with good, we protect ourselves and all those involved from acting unjustly.

Secondly, if an evil act has indeed been carried out with ill intent, we still benefit from responding with that which is better. It saves us from retaliating with an evil equal to the one enacted against us, or worse, an evil that is greater than the one being avenged thus leading us to behave unjustly. Additionally, and perhaps most importantly, if this is a person who despite their ill intent has consciousness of Allah and goodness in their hearts—for no one is perfect and we are all capable of erring—your gracious response may snap them out of their stupor of malice and deliver them to remorse and rectification. It may even deliver them to friendship and devotion as Allah suggests in the verse above. It should be noted that if a person has acted with evil and ill intent then to respond with 'good' doesn't mean that one should simply roll over and be compliant, especially if the evil is an act of *shirk* or injustice. In such a case, the Muslim must be activated into a response that is good in that it seeks to remove these ills from society.

Allah notes that this is no easy task, and that indeed it is not the good fortune of all to be able to respond to evil with good. It is only for those who have patience and those who have been granted such good fortitude from Allah. Perhaps the greatest example of this from the life of ʿĀ'ishah ﷺ is with regards to the slander that she had to endure, the lessons from which are many—and so have their own chapter in this book. From the life of the Prophet ﷺ his patience and reliance on Allah at Ṭā'if is indisputably one that is also rich with such lessons.

As is well known, when the Prophet ﷺ was first commissioned by Allah to spread the word of Islam in Makkah, he was met by mockery which soon turned into hostility as the message with which he came began to shake the throne of those in power. The nascent Muslim community found itself boycotted, displaced and tortured. Years of oppressive hardship descended upon the Muslim community and were marked by two of the greatest tragedies of the Prophet's life: the death of his uncle, Abū Ṭālib, and the death of his beloved wife, the honourable Khadijah ﷺ. This year was to become known as 'the Year of Sadness'.

At this destitute moment, the Prophet ﷺ sought out allies. He set out to Ṭā'if hopeful for a friend in this time of loneliness, a shelter against the storm of cruelty. When he arrived at Ṭā'if he spoke to each of the three chieftains in the city, but each repelled him. He reached out to the townsfolk, but they too reviled him with such contempt that when he was made to leave the town, they set the children of the town loose to pelt the noble Prophet ﷺ with stones and sticks. Beloved Muhammad ﷺ, beleaguered and heartbroken, took rest in a nearby garden. He removed his shoes to reveal feet bloodied by the attack and cried out in anguish to his Lord saying:

> O Allah! To You alone do I complain of my weakness and the lack of my abilities and my humiliation before the people. O Most Merciful of those who show Mercy! You are the Lord of the weak and You are my Lord. To whom do you leave me? To someone distant who attacks me? To an enemy to whom you have given control over my affairs? As long as You are not angry with me, I do not care [about their actions], but Your protection is sufficient, ample for me. I seek refuge in the Divine Light of your Countenance which illuminates all darkness, and by which all affairs of this world and the hereafter are made right, may it never be that I incur Your anger nor that You should be displeased with me. I will implore You until You are pleased. There is no power, and there is no might except Yours.

Truly it would be enough to stop at this *duʿā'*. It would suffice as a lesson in responding to evil with good, but this is Muhammad ﷺ, the best of all creation; his example extends beyond this *duʿā'*. Just as our hearts are moved by this scene played out in our imaginations, it shook the heavens too, and caused the Angel Jibrāʾīl ﷺ to descend immediately. He greeted the sorrowful Prophet ﷺ and said to him, 'Allah knows all that has passed between you and these people. He has stationed an angel in charge of the mountains [on either side of Ṭāʾif] to be at your command.' At this, the angel stationed at the mountains was brought forward and he spoke to the Prophet ﷺ, 'Messenger of Allah, I am at your service. If you wish, I can cause the mountains overlooking this town to collide with each other, so that all the people therein will be crushed to death, or you may suggest any other punishment for them.'

How often have we been wronged and wished for such powerful vengeance that both satisfied our anger and sent out a message? And what was it that the Prophet ﷺ responded with when such power was made possible for him? He replied graciously, 'Even if these people do not accept Islam, I do hope from Allah that amongst their progeny there will be those who will worship Allah and serve His way.' This was the noble and exemplary way of the Prophet ﷺ driven by love for Allah and not the ego, motivated by the promise of Jannah and not worldly repute and leadership. But as Allah most High tells us, this wisdom, patience, and forbearance is not the fortune of everyone. May Allah make us of those granted such success and good fortune, *āmīn*.

The Prophet's *duʿāʾ* for his *ummah*

ʿĀʾishah ❧ reported: 'When I saw the Prophet ❧ with a cheerful face, I said, Messenger of Allah, supplicate to Allah for me. The Prophet ❧ said, "O Allah, forgive ʿĀʾishah for her past and future sins, done in secret and in public."' ʿĀʾishah ❧ laughed so much that her head fell from his lap. The Prophet ❧ said to her, 'Does my supplication make you happy?' ʿĀʾishah ❧ said, 'Why would your supplication not make me happy?' The Prophet ❧ said, 'By Allah, it is my supplication for my nation in every prayer.'[86]

Umm al-Muʾminīn, ʿĀʾishah ❧ was always eager in attaining the favours of Allah and the Messenger of Allah ❧, and so it was her habit that when she would see the Prophet ❧ in a cheerful mood she would ask him to supplicate for her. This hadith paints a portrait of matrimonial harmony, a loving scene between the Prophet ❧ and his cherished wife, sitting in private with ʿĀʾishah's head cradled in the lap of the Prophet ❧. He, in turn smiling, gentle and good humoured towards his wife, moving her to ask him to make *duʿāʾ* for her knowing that at this moment the happiness in his heart will deliver to his tongue an auspicious and invaluable supplication in her favour. When the Prophet ❧ utters those words of forgiveness for all of ʿĀʾishah's sins, she is so happy she becomes giddy with joy.

We too should be filled with giddy joy because it is the same *duʿāʾ* the Prophet ﷺ made for us. That this is the petition of the Prophet ﷺ before God for us as well is a source of not just joy but also comfort for each of us. It is only natural that this would be the *duʿāʾ* of the Prophet ﷺ for us when Allah has described him to us saying: *A Messenger has come to you from among yourselves. Your suffering distresses him; he is deeply concerned for you and full of kindness and mercy towards the believers* (*al-Tawbah* 9: 128). Regarding this verse, Imam al-Qurṭubī cites a beautiful reflection by al-Ḥusayn ibn al-Faḍl who said, 'Allah does not combine for any of the Prophets two names from amongst His own Names except for the Prophet Muhammad ﷺ. He said [regarding the Prophet] that he is "full of kindness (*ra'ūfun*) and mercy (*raḥīm*) towards the believers," and He has said [about Himself], *Indeed Allah is most full of kindness (ra'ūfun) and mercy (raḥīm) towards humankind* (*al-ḥajj* 22: 65).' Allah chose for Himself the pairing of the attributes of kindness and mercy and then cloaked the Prophet ﷺ alone out of all the prophets, in the same combination.

This supplication is not an isolated moment; this was a *duʿāʾ* fixed on the tongue of the Prophet ﷺ and one to which he will remain committed even beyond his earthly life. In a hadith recorded in Muslim, the Prophet ﷺ is reported to have said, 'Allah has given one *duʿāʾ* to every single prophet and every single messenger, which He has guaranteed He will respond to. Every single prophet has used up this *duʿā'* for himself in this world, except for me. I have saved it and I have not used it and I will not use it in this life. I have kept it for my *ummah* and I will use it for them on the Day of Judgement. And my *duʿā'* will be, "O Allah, forgive my entire *ummah*."'

6

At the first sign of hardship the believer's refuge is in Allah

Zaynab bint Jaḥsh ﵂ and ʿĀ'ishah ﵂ were in a playful exchange with each other over their respective status with Allah. Zaynab boasted about her marriage being validated from above the sky, while ʿĀ'ishah ﵂ responded, 'I was the one for whom exoneration was revealed in His Book when Ibn al-Muʿaṭṭal carried me on his ride.' Zaynab ﵂ asked ʿĀ'ishah ﵂ what she said at that time, and ʿĀ'ishah ﵂ replied, 'I said: *ḥasbi Allah wa niʿmal wakeel*,

حَسْبِي اللهُ وَنِعْمَ الْوَكِيلُ

Allah is sufficient for me and what an excellent Disposer of affairs [is He].'[87]

What appears to be a nondescript conversation between two wives of the Prophet ﷺ, carries within it reference to one of the most tumultuous times in the life of ʿĀ'ishah, that brought with it many lessons for the Muslim community for generations to come. In an uncharacteristically long narration recorded in *ṣaḥīḥ al-Bukhārī*, ʿĀ'ishah relays the events of what was to become known as, *ḥadīth al-Ifk*, the Incident of the Slander.[88] She details how when the Prophet ﷺ would intend to make a journey, he would draw lots amongst his wives to decide on who would accompany him. On one such occasion, it was ʿĀ'ishah's lot that was drawn and so she accompanied the Prophet ﷺ as he went out to battle. She reports being seated in a palanquin that was lifted and placed on a camel to maintain her privacy during travel. The battle was a success, and the caravan was returning to Madinah. On the journey back they took a break. ʿĀ'ishah's palanquin was dismounted from her camel and she took the opportunity to disembark and relieve herself. When she returned, she realised that the necklace she had been wearing had fallen, so she retraced her footsteps in the hopes of finding it. Having retrieved her necklace, ʿĀ'ishah hurried back to where the army had camped only to find they had reassembled and had continued without her. Those who had been charged with returning the palanquin of ʿĀ'ishah back to the camel had not noticed it was empty due to how little she weighed.

Perturbed but confident that they would soon realise their mistake and come find her, ʿĀ'ishah decided to sit and wait for the caravan to return. Whilst she waited, fatigue overcame her, and she lay down and fell asleep. Sometime later she was awoken by the voice of a man saying, '*Innā lillāhi wa innā ilayhi rājiʿūn*. Verily, from Allah we come and to Allah do we return.' She recognised the young soldier as Ṣafwān ibn al-Muʿaṭṭal, and he recognised her as ʿĀ'ishah, Mother of the Believers. He had been tasked with staying behind the army convoy to ensure nothing was left behind as they travelled through the desert. Ṣafwān simply dismounted his camel and brought it to kneel so that ʿĀ'ishah could mount it. No further words were exchanged as he led the camel back to Madinah. ʿĀ'ishah recalls that her and Ṣafwān ended up overtaking the army that had taken another stop in its journey and so arrived at the city before the Prophet ﷺ and his army did. It did not take long for the hypocrites in the city to seize upon the sight of the young wife of the Prophet ﷺ known to be his dearest wife, travelling upon a camel being led by a handsome young soldier and to conjure from that the most hurtful and slanderous lies. This was a gift for the adversaries of Islam wishing to cause dissent in the household of the Prophet ﷺ, agony in his heart, disrepute upon ʿĀ'ishah and scandal amongst the Muslims.

Remarkably though, on her return to Madinah, ʿĀ'ishah had fallen terribly ill and taken to her bed. Whilst the city outside was ablaze with gossip, ʿĀ'ishah remained in her room entirely unaware. The only clue she had was the distance in the Prophet's demeanour. She recalls, 'I wasn't aware of anything about [the rumours], but I felt in my ill state I was not getting the usual attentiveness from the Messenger of Allah that I would get when I was ill. He would simply come in and ask, "How is she?" And then leave.'

It was not until some days later that she was to hear from the mother of Misṭaḥ, her cousin who was involved in spreading the rumour, that she realised what was being said. ʿĀ'ishah was overcome by the distress of what she had heard and felt her condition worsen as a result. She asked the Prophet permission to be excused to go stay with her parents. He granted her this request, delivering her to her parents. ʿĀ'ishah had wished to go to them to verify what she had heard. Her mother, Umm Ruman, sought to console ʿĀ'ishah, brushing it off as part of the territory of being a beautiful and beloved wife with detractors among the community and co-wives. '*Subḥān Allah*!' ʿĀ'ishah responded, astounded that the people could be casting such aspersion on her fidelity and character. She wept all night and all day, inconsolable at the treachery she was experiencing from the community.

In the meantime, the Prophet ﷺ too nursed a wounded heart. ʿĀ'ishah ﷺ, his most adored wife, had come into the crosshairs of the hypocrites and those with diseased hearts, who were busily stoking the fires of gossip ravaging Madinah. He decided to turn to trusted Companions for their perspectives, worried no doubt that his love for ʿĀ'ishah ﷺ may prevent him from having clarity on the matter, and perhaps also in search of something to console him, to prove that the rumours were false. He turned to Usāmah ibn Zayd ﷺ and Ali ibn Abī Ṭālib ﷺ, asking them what they thought of the rumours and whether he should consider divorce. Usāmah ﷺ responded in defence of ʿĀ'ishah ﷺ, stating, 'She is your wife and we do not know anything about her except good.' Ali ﷺ responded, 'O Allah's Messenger, Allah does not put you in difficulty and there are plenty of other women apart from her. But if you wish to know, then ask her maidservant; she will tell you the truth.'

At this prompt, the Prophet ﷺ called upon Barīrah, the maidservant Ali ﷺ had mentioned, and asked her what she had witnessed of ʿĀ'ishah's character, and if there had been any behaviour that raised suspicions in her about ʿĀ'ishah. Barīrah responded in earnest about ʿĀ'ishah ﷺ, saying to the Prophet ﷺ, 'By the One who has sent you with the Truth, I have never seen anything disagreeable in her, except that she is a young girl who forgets and goes to sleep having left the dough uncovered so then the goats come and eat it.' The only criticism Barīrah could muster about ʿĀʾishah ❧ was a mere symptom of the carefree naivety of youth.

Amongst those who had partaken in spreading the slander against ʿĀʾishah ❧ was Ḥamnah bint Jaḥsh ❧, the sister of Zaynab bint Jaḥsh ❧, so the Prophet ❧ went to her too to enquire what she knew of ʿĀʾishah ❧. Zaynab ❧ had also replied in much the same way as Barīrah. She said, 'Allah's Messenger, I refrain from claiming falsely that I have heard or seen anything. By Allah, I know nothing except good [about ʿĀʾishah].' Emboldened by the positive testimonies, the Prophet ❧ took to the pulpit and chastised his people, stating 'I swear by Allah! I know nothing except good about my family and they have blamed a man [Ṣafwān ibn al-Muʿaṭṭal] about whom I know nothing except good and he never used to enter my home unless with me.' The brotherhood that Islam had so miraculously delivered warring tribes to, had been threatened in the climate of subterfuge and mistrust that now festered with the people either siding with or against ʿĀʾishah ❧. And so even as the Companions sought to allay the worries of the Prophet ❧, they ended up opening up old tribal schisms, and chaos descended amongst them. The Prophet ❧ called for quiet. A heavy burdensome silence fell, and it was another month before anything was going to change.

ʿĀʾishah ❧ reports her days passing in woe, her nights passing without sleep, and her tears flowing endlessly such that she recalled, 'I thought my liver would burst from all my weeping.' Indeed, an atmosphere of mourning engulfed ʿĀʾishah 🌸 and her parents' home. A woman from amongst the Anṣār came to visit, and as she sat next to ʿĀʾishah 🌸 she began to cry with her. In this moment, the Prophet 🌸 entered upon them, bade them *salām*, then came and sat with them—the first time since the slander had taken over the community. He addressed his wife and said:

> Āʾishah, I have heard what is being said about you. If you are innocent then Allah will absolve you, and if you are guilty of a sin then seek Allah's forgiveness and turn to Him in repentance. Indeed, if a servant of Allah recognises their wrongdoing and then turns to Allah [in repentance], then Allah turns towards them [in mercy].

Perhaps ʿĀʾishah 🌸 had wanted to hear words of confidence and assurance from her husband. Perhaps after a month of agony and no discussion, she had imagined her husband would come to her aid no matter what and stand by her unquestioningly—not come to her with the position of a stranger left to balance the words of the people against hers, because the moment those words passed his lips, ʿĀʾishah 🌸 says her tears ran dry.

Instead of arriving with words of support and confidence, the Prophet 🌸 had come with the words of an impartial onlooker. His position as leader of the Madinans demanded it of him. He was the man who had so boldly stated that even if his beloved daughter Fatima 🌸 was guilty of stealing, he would apply the penal code of the time upon her and cut her hand off because justice and fairness must overcome nepotism and favouritism. But when he uttered those words, he likely never imagined having to contend with the possibility of the infidelity of his love.

ʿĀ'ishah 🌸 turned to her father and asked him to respond on her behalf, but he lowered his gaze, words failing him. ʿĀ'ishah 🌸 turned to her mother and implored her to speak on her behalf to the Prophet 🌸, but she too replied deflated, 'I don't know what to say to Allah's Messenger.' With neither her husband nor her parents' confidence, ʿĀ'ishah 🌸 had to look within herself for strength. She recalls that she was relatively young then and not particularly well-versed in the Qur'an, but she mustered the strength she needed. She addressed them all saying:

By Allah, I know that you have heard what has been said and it has embedded itself in your hearts as truth, so now if I tell you that I am innocent you will not believe me, and if I confess to you [that I am guilty], even though Allah knows my innocence, you will believe that. By Allah, I find no fitting similitude for

> me and you except that of Yūsuf's father who said, 'Verily for me is a beautiful patience that is most fitting against what you assert. It is Allah alone whose Help is sought.'

She then lay down on her bed and turned her back on them, full of conviction that Allah knew the truth and that her reliance would be on Allah alone. In this state, she hoped for the Prophet ﷺ to be granted a dream in which Allah might show him a vision that would exonerate her. She said, 'By Allah, I never thought that Allah would reveal Divine inspiration about my case that would be recited forever as I considered myself unworthy of such a thing,' but Allah had a greater response in store for her. Before the Prophet ﷺ could rise to leave, he was seized by the state he was known to enter when receiving Divine revelation. Sweat was dripping from his noble face and body like pearls, despite the chill in the air, and when he was finally released from the moment, he smiled broadly and proclaimed with joy and relief, 'O ʿĀ'ishah! Allah has declared your innocence!' ʿĀ'ishah's mother sharing the joy and relief of the Prophet ﷺ, prompted her daughter to get up and go to her husband. But ʿĀ'ishah ؓ replied, 'By Allah, I will not go to him, and I praise none but Allah.' It was on this occasion that Allah revealed verses 11 to 20 in Surah al-Noor.

I end this book with this story for it encompasses all of the lessons and wisdoms imparted throughout the pages that precede it: the reward of patience for the one who finds no Helper nor Aid but Allah, who turns to Allah with full conviction of the Truth. The promise for the one who finds themselves entirely abandoned and overwhelmed by the magnitude of their burden, that Allah is your Comforting Friend. The evidence that when relief comes it is so great that the burden you once thought may kill you becomes a test for which you become grateful because through it you gained so much that it is as if the test never came. It is a testimony to Allah's care, concern, and elevation of the weak, especially women. It is a story of holding strong to the Rope of Allah, to adhering to the truth even when none are inclined to believe you, and to continually return with each injury to supplicate to Allah. It is the promise of Allah that indeed, with every hardship come multiple eases, and that justice and truth always triumph in the end.

Endnotes

1. Brother to the more widely known Companion, Abū Mūsā al-Ashʿarī.
2. al-Afghani, S. *ʿAisha wa al-Siyāsah* p. 14.
3. Masrūq ibn al-Ajdaʿ a second generation *Tābiʿī* was a respected jurist and transmitter of ḥadith.
4. ʿAisha Geissinger, "ʿAisha bint Abu Bakr and Her Contributions to the Formation of the Islamic Tradition', *Religion Compass*, 5/1 (2011), pp. 37–49.
5. For more on this, you may reference my forthcoming book, *Gendering the Hadith Tradition: Recentering the Authority of Aisha, Mother of the Believers* due to be published in 2023 by Oxford University Press.
6. *Tafsīr* of (*al-Baqarah* 2: 186) in *Tafsīr al-Qur'ān al-'Aẓīm* by Ibn Kathīr and *Jāmiʿ al-Bayān ʿan Ta'wīl āy al-Qur'an* by al-Ṭabarī.
7. Salmān al-Fārsi reported: 'The Prophet ﷺ said, "Verily, Allah is munificent and generous. He would be shy, when a man raises his hands to Him, to turn them away empty and disappointed."' (*Sunan al-Tirmidhī*)
8. *Tafsīr* of (*al-Baqarah* 2: 284) in *Tafsīr al-Kabīr* by Fakhr al-Dīn al-Rāzi.
9. *ṣaḥīḥ al-Bukhārī*, Book of *Tafsīr*.
10. *ṣaḥīḥ al-Bukhārī*, Book of Patience.
11. *Tafsīr* of (*al-Baqarah* 2: 224) in *Fatḥ al-Qadīr* by al-Shawkāni.
12. *Jāmiʿ al-Tirmidhī*, in the chapter on Zuhd.
13. Reported in the *tafsīr* of (*al-Mā'idah* 5: 67) in *Tafsīr al-Ṭabarī* and *Tafsīr al-Qurṭubī*, *Tafsīr Ibn Kathīr*.
14. Imam al-Ṭabarī in *al-Jāmiʿ li Aḥkām al-Qur'an* and al-Tirmidhī, Chapters on *Tafsīr* - both acknowledge

weakness in the transmission of this hadith. The story is also narrated by Ibn Kathīr and Imam al-Shawkānī in their respective *tafsīr*s of this verse without noting any weakness in the chain. Either way the lesson is sound.

15. *ṣidāq* is often translated as *mahr*, the dowry, but it is important to note that the word *ṣidāq* entails far more than just dowry. It also entails truthfulness, honesty, love, affection, friendship, and loyalty, all of which are essential ingredients to a successful marriage built on the foundations of mindfulness of Allah.
16. For more on this see also, *Believing Women in Islam* by Asma Barlas, p. 223 and Ayesha S Chaudhry in *Men in Charge? Rethinking Authority in Muslim Legal Tradition* edited by Ziba Mir-Hossein, Mulki al-Sharmani and Jana Rumminger.
17. *ṣaḥ*īḥ of Abū ḥātim ibn ḥibbān.
18. *ṣaḥ*īḥ al-Bukh*ārī* Book of Manāqib.
19. *ṣaḥ*īḥ Muslim The Book of Menstruation.
20. *ṣaḥīḥ Muslim,* The Book of Menstruation.
21. For some insight into this, see, Yusuff, A. 2021. Between hair and hijab: Black British Muslim women on their relationship with Afro hair. *The New Arab* [Online] 22nd October. Available from: https://english.alaraby.co.uk/features/hair-vs-hijab-black-british-muslim-women-and-afro-style?amp
22. *Al-Ijābah* by al-Zarkashi.
23. See, Fatima Mernissi, *The Veil and the Male Elite: A Feminist Interpretation of Women's Rights in Islam*, tr. by Mary J. Lakeland (Reading, 1991).
24. 'The worst of the three,' means the worst party out of the mother and father who commit adultery and the child that is born as a result of it.
25. *Al-Ijābah* by al-Zarkashi.
26. *ṣaḥīḥ Muslim*, The Book of Masājid and Places of Prayer, in the chapter, 'Who is Most Entitled to Lead the Prayer'.

27. *Al-Ijābah* by al-Zarkashi.

28. *ṣaḥīḥ al-Bukhārī*, The Book of Prayers, in the chapter 'A Person Facing Another Person Whilst Praying'.

29. In *ṣaḥīḥ al-Bukhārī*, The Book of Prayers, ʿĀʾishah ✿ is recorded as saying, 'The things which annul the prayers were mentioned to me. They said, "Prayer is annulled by a dog, a donkey, and a woman [if they pass in front of someone praying]." I said, "You have made us [women] dogs. The Prophet ✿ used to pray while I used to lie in my bed between him and the *qiblah*…".'

30. *ṣaḥīḥ Muslim*, The Book of Prayers of the Travellers.

31. In Surah al-Fajr, verse 28, Allah describes how the believers will be called back to their Lord with the beautiful words, 'Return to your Lord, well-pleased and pleasing [to Allah].'

32. *ṣaḥīḥ al-Bukhārī*, The Book of *Raqāiq*

33. *ṣaḥīḥ Muslim*, The Book of Fasting, in chapter, 'The Virtue of Ṣuḥūr and The Virtue of Hastening to Break Fast'.

34. "Indeed Allah wishes for you ease, and not hardship…" *Surah al-Baqarah* 2: 185

35. *Sunan Abū Dāwūd*, The Book of Clothing.

36. For those curious about the varying attitudes of Muslims towards dogs over history, *The Superiority of Dogs Over Many of Those Who Wear Clothes* by the tenth-century scholar Ibn al-Marzubān provides an unusual and contrasting position to the prevalent contemporary Muslim attitude towards dogs.

37. *Musnad Aḥmad*

38. *Al-Ijābah* by al-Zarkashi

39. *Sunan Abū Dāwūd*, The Book of Clothing.

40. *Al-Ijābah* by al-Zarkashi

41. *ṣaḥīḥ Muslim*, The Book of *Raqāiq* and *Zuhd*

42. *Al-Ijābah* by al-Zarkashi

43. *Al-Ijābah* by al-Zarkashi

44. See below the hadith on Gentleness for more on this story.

45. *ṣaḥīḥ Muslim* and *Sunan al-Nasā'ī*
46. *Sunan ibn Mājah,* The Book of *Zuhd*
47. Gitanjali by Rabindranath Tagore
48. Nabia Abbott, *Aisha: The Beloved of Muhammed* (Chicago, 1942) 108.
49. Labīd ibn Rabī'ah was a highly acclaimed poet among the Arabs. His was one of the seven poems famously known as *al-Mu'allaqāt* which hung in the Kaaba in the period before Islam. These poems are considered to form the foundation of all Arabic poetry. He converted to Islam at an advanced age, when he had come to Madinah upon an errand for his uncle. During his time in Madinah it is said he was struck by the shortest surah of the Qur'an, Surah al-Kawthar, and consequently he and his whole family embraced Islam.
50. *al-ʿIqd al-Farīd* Vol. 2, 187
51. Al-ṭabarī, *The History of al-ṭabarī*, Vol. 16
52. Wilfred Madelung, *The Succession to Muhammad*, p. 160.
53. A reference to Surah Āl ʿImrān 3: 102–103
54. Meaning to kill her as ʿUthman was killed.
55. (*āl ʿImrān* 3: 23)
56. *Tārīkh al-Ṭabarī* Vol 16, pp. 74-76
57. *Al-Imtā' wa al-Muʿānasa* by Abū Ḥayyān al-Tawhīdī, Vol. 3, p. 199.
58. *al-ʿIqd al-Farīd*, Vol. 1, p. 89.
59. *Al-Mu'jam al-Awsat* 5884
60. *Tārīkh al-Ṭabarī,* Vol. 16, pp. 135–136.
61. Ibid. p. 149.
62. *al-ʿIqd al-Farīd,* Vol. 1, p. 57.
63. *ṣaḥīḥ al-Bukhārī*, The Book of Virtues and Merits of the Prophet and his Companions and the *Muwaṭṭa* of Imam Mālik, The Book of Good Character.
64. *Riyāḍ al-ṣāliḥīn*, The Book of Virtues.
65. *Al-Adab al-Mufrad,* al-Bukhārī, The Book of Looking After Children.
66. *ṣaḥīḥ al-Bukhārī*, The Book of Revelation.

67. *Al-Shamā'il al-Muhammadiyyah*, Imam al-Tirmidhī, What the Messenger of Allah ﷺ Ate With Bread.
68. *ṣaḥīḥ al-Bukhārī*, The Book of Good Manners, in the chapter,' To Be Good to Neighbours', and *al-Adab al-Mufrad*, The Book of Neighbours.
69. *Al-Adab al-Mufrad,* The Book of Dealing with People and Good Character.
70. *Al-Adab al-Mufrad*, The Book of Compassion.
71. *ṣaḥīḥ ibn ḥibbān.*
72. *The Masnavi*, Jalāl al-Dīn al-Rūmī, translated by Jawid Mojaddedi, Book One, p. 104.
73. *ṣaḥīḥ Muslim*, The Book of Virtue, Enjoining Good Manners and Maintaining Ties of Kinship, Chapter, The Virtue of Gentleness.
74. *ṣaḥīḥ Muslim*
75. *Jāmiʿ al-Tirmidhī*, in the chapter on Supplication
76. Allah states in Surah al-Furqān, verse 63: *The true servants of the Merciful One are those who walk on the earth gently and when the foolish ones address them, they simply say: "Peace to you".*
77. *Al-ʿIqd al-Farīd*, Vol. 5, p. 19
78. Allah states in Surah al-Tawbah verse 40: *If you will not aid him, Allah certainly aided him when those who disbelieved expelled him, he being* ***the second of the two****, when they were both in the cave, when he said to his companion: Grieve not, surely Allah is with us. So Allah sent down His tranquillity upon him and strengthened him with hosts which you did not see, and made lowest the word of those who disbelieved; and the word of Allah, that is the highest; and Allah is Mighty, Wise.*
79. In *Sunan al-Tirmidhī*, the Prophet ﷺ is recorded as saying, 'Abu Bakr is in Paradise. Umar is in Paradise. Uthman is in Paradise. Ali is in Paradise. Ṭalḥah is in Paradise. Al-Zubayr is in Paradise. ʿAbd al-Raḥmān ibn ʿAwf is in Paradise. Saʿd is in Paradise. Saʿīd is in Paradise. Abū ʿUbaydah ibn al-Jarrāh is in Paradise.'

80. See *Ibrāhīm* 14: 16, *al-Kahf* 18: 29, *al-Dukhān* 44: 45, *al-Maʿārij* 70: 8.
81. *Musnad Aḥmad.*
82. *Al-Adab al-Mufrad,* The Book of Supplication
83. A *ḥadīth qudsīi* recorded in *ṣaḥīḥ Muslim* states: Allah Almighty says, 'Whoever comes with a good deed will have the reward of ten like it and even more. Whoever comes with an evil deed will be recompensed for one evil deed like it or he will be forgiven. Whoever draws close to Me by the length of a hand, I will draw close to him by the length of an arm. Whoever draws close to Me by the length of an arm, I will draw close to him by the length of a fathom. Whoever comes to Me walking, I will come to him running. Whoever meets Me with enough sins to fill the earth, not associating any partners with Me, I will meet him with as much forgiveness.'
84. *Riyāḍ al-ṣāliḥīn*, The Book of Virtues.
85. *Jāmiʿ al-Tirmidhī*, in the chapter on 'Righteousness and Maintaining Good Relations with Kinfolk'.
86. *ṣaḥīḥ Ibn ḥibbān.*
87. *Tafsīr Jāmiʿ al-Bayān fi Tafsīr al-Qur'an*, al-Ṭabarī Verse 24:11.
88. *ṣaḥīḥ al-Bukhārī*, The Book of Tafsīr.

Bibliography

Arabic References

Ibn ʿAbd Rabbihi al-Andalusī, Aḥmad ibn Muhammad. 2008. *al-ʿIqd al-Farīd*. Beirut: Dār al-Kutub al-ʿIlmiyyah.

Al-Afghānī, S. *ʿā'ishah wa al-Siyāsah.*

Al-Bayhaqī, Aḥmad ibn al-Ḥusayn ibn ʿAlī. 2003 *Sunan al-Bayhaqī al-Kubrā*. Dār al-Kutub al-ʿIlmiyyah.

Al-Bukhārī, Muḥammad ibn Ismaʿīl. 2002. *ṣaḥīḥ al-Bukhārī*. Damascus: Dār ibn Kathīr.

Al-Dhahabī, Muḥammad ibn Aḥmad. *Siyar Aʿlām al-Nubalā'*. Beirut: Mu'asasah al-Risālah.

Al-Ḥākim, Muḥammad ibn ʿAbdullah. 2002. *al-Mustadrak ʿAlā al-ṣaḥīḥayn*. Beirut: Dār al-Kutub al-ʿIlmiyyah.

Ibn Ḥajar al-ʿAsqalānī, Aḥmad ibn ʿAlī ibn Muḥammad. n.d. *Fatḥ al-Bārī bi–Sharḥ ṣaḥīḥ al-Bukhārī*. Riyadh: Bayt al-Afkār al-Dawliyyah.

Ibn Ḥanbal, Aḥmad ibn Muḥammad. 2009. *Musnad al-Imam Aḥmad ibn ḥanbal*. Beirut: Mu'assasah al-Risālah.

Ibn Ḥibbān, Abū ḥātim. 1952. *ṣaḥīḥ Ibn ḥibbān*. Egypt: Dār al-Maʿārif.

Ibn Kathīr, Ismaʿīl ibn ʿUmar. 1999. *Tafsīr al-Qur'ān al-ʿAẓīm*. Dār al-ṭayyibah.

Muslim, Muslim ibn al-Ḥajjāj. 2006. *ṣaḥīḥ Muslim*. Dār al-Ṭayyibah.

Al-Nasā'ī, Aḥmad ibn ʿAlī. *Sunan Al-Nasā'ī,* 2015. Riyadh: Dār al-Ḥaḍārah.

Al-Qurtubī, ibn ʿAbd al-Barr. 1994. *Jāmiʿ Bayān al-ʿIlm wa Faḍlih*. Damaam: Dār ibn al-Jawzī.

Al-Rāzī, Fakhr al-Dīn. 2008. *al-Tafsīr al-Kabīr*. Beirut: Dār al-Fikr.

Al-Shawkānī, Muḥammad ibn ʿAlī ibn Muḥammad. 2009. *Fatḥ al-Qadīr*. Dār al-Mu'ayyad.

Al-Ṭabarī Muḥammad ibn Jarīr. 1994. *Jāmiʿ al-Bayān ʿan Ta'wīl āy al-Qur'ān*. Beirut: Mu'assasah al-Risālah.

Al-Tawḥīdī, Abū ḥayyān. 2004 *Al-Imtā' wa al-Mu'ānasah*. Beirut: al-Maktabah al-ʿAṣṣariyyah.
Al-Tirmidhī Muḥammad ibn ʿīsa. 1996. *Jāmiʿ al-Tirmidhī*. Dār al-Gharb al-Islāmī.
Al-Zarkashī Badr al-Dīn Abū ʿAbdullah Muḥammad ibn ʿAbdullah ibn Bahādur. 2004. *al-Ijābah li-īrādi mā Istadrakatuhu ʿā'ishah ʿalā al-ṣahābah*, edited by Mehmet Bünyamen Arül. Beirut: Mu'assasah al-Risālah.

English References

Abbott, N., *Aishah: The Beloved of Mohammed* (London: Al Saqi, 1985).
Madelung, W., *The Succession to Muhammad: A Study of the Early Caliphate* (Cambridge: Cambridge University Press, 1994).
Al-Rūmī, J., *The Masnavi* tr. by Jawid Mojaddedi (Oxford: Oxford University Press, 2008).
Al-Ṭabarī, *The History of al-ṭabarī* (New York: State University of New York Press, 1997).
Tagore, R., *Gitanjali Digireads.com*.

Index